Standing with the Poor

Standing with the Poor

Theological Reflections on Economic Reality

Edited by Paul Plenge Parker
Illustrated by Brian Bakke

Contributors
David G. Buttrick
James H. Cone
Greg J. Duncan
Ronald Goetz
Jacquelyn Grant
Martha S. Hill
Saul D. Hoffman
Jorge L. Morales
Gail R. O'Day
Wallace Charles Smith
June Alliman Yoder

The Pilgrim Press
Cleveland, Ohio

The Pilgrim Press, Cleveland, Ohio 44115

© 1992 by The Pilgrim Press

Unless otherwise noted, biblical quotations are from the New Revised Standard
Version of the Bible, © 1989 by the Division of Christian Education of the National
Council of the Churches of Christ in the U.S.A., and are used by permission.
Quotations noted NEB are from the New English Bible, © by the Delegates of the
Oxford University Press and the Syndics of the Cambridge University Press 1961,
1970. Quotations noted Jerusalem Bible, © 1966, 1967, and 1968 by Darton,
Longman & Todd Ltd. and Doubleday & Company, Inc.

Printed in the United States of America
The paper used in this publication is acid free and meets the minimum requirements of
American National Standard for Information Sciences-Permanence of Paper for
Printed Library Materials, ANSI Z39.48–1984

97 96 95 94 93 92   5 4 3 2 1

Library of Congress Cataloging-in-Publication Data

Standing with the poor : theological reflections on economic reality /
contributors David G. Buttrick...[et al.] ; edited by Paul Plenge
Parker ; illustrated by Brian Bakke.
p.   cm.
ISBN 0–8298–0926–0
1. Church work with the poor—United States. 2. United States—
Social conditions—1980– I. Buttrick, David G., 1927–
II. Parker, Paul Plenge.
BV639.P6S73   1992
261.8'325'097309048—dc20   92–36254
CIP

To G. H. S.
teacher and friend

Contents

Illustrations

Foreword

This is a timely book. The collapse of Soviet and Eastern European socialism has forced a sober reexamination of economic assumptions around the world. This book will contribute to that reexamination among Christians.

At first glance, it appears that the use of government as an instrument of economic justice and social welfare has been discredited. It appears that Adam Smith's theory of the "invisible hand" has at last triumphed and that we now know for sure that the best way to deal with poverty is to encourage competitive individualism in economics. It appears that the only hope for the poor is the overall improvement of the economy, which only free competition can promise. And it appears that poor people themselves, through their social irresponsibility, are responsible for their own poverty. As one Reagan-era writer put it, "In order to succeed, the poor need most of all the spur of their poverty."[1] The revolutionary developments in Eastern Europe and the sweeping political successes of Reaganism in America (and Thatcherism in Great Britain) enhance the appearance that this is the right perspective on poverty.

But appearances can be deceiving. For one thing, the Eastern countries are themselves in considerable turmoil. While they have wisely repudiated the totalitarianism of the past half-century, it is not at all clear yet that the former socialist societies should pin all their hopes on laissez-faire economics to solve social welfare problems. From

Poland to Bulgaria and from Czechoslovakia to Estonia, these countries are struggling with unemployment and a host of other economic difficulties. It is far too early to proclaim the triumph of free market economics as a sufficient solution.

One does not have to turn to Eastern Europe to learn that. The sweeping political successes of Reaganism in America have not been paralleled by economic accomplishment. Superficially, the 1980s were a decade of remarkable economic recovery. Actually, the recovery was funded by enormous trade deficits and a yawning imbalance of the federal budget. We can leave the fine points of that to the economists. Even if the recovery was itself healthy, it simply did not "deliver" for the poor people of America. Despite eight years of economic growth, the number of poor people remained fairly constant at around 33 million. Whatever the increases in national wealth during that period, very little trickled down to the poor. To cite a favorite metaphor from the 1980s, the rising economic tide did not raise all boats.

This book is timely because it is published exactly when the illusions have become clear to large numbers of people. In part, this may simply be because of middle-class self-interest. Those who face dramatic rises in health care costs, great job insecurity, and a less hopeful future may not, for such reasons, be more sympathetic to the plight of the poor. But at least they are more likely to address the hard economic questions more critically. In such a climate Christian thought can raise the deeper value questions.

I am impressed by a growing awareness in this society of the moral bankruptcy of the economic culture of the 1980s. The "greed is good" mentality is not finally good economics either; at the social and cultural level it is ruinous. Our country has been torn apart by its inability to focus on common purpose. The great economic contribution of the 1980s was to make some people very rich. But that is not good enough. Too many people remained poor, and the large middle segment of the society was left no better than before.

To me, the compelling contribution of this book is its reminder that no society can exist with health if many of its members are disregarded. Poor people may be a relatively small minority in the affluent North American and European context, but they are the weak link in the chain where the character of the whole community is tested. So long as their material well-being is neglected, the moral health of the whole community is diminished.

That point is not a new one for Christians to make. It is pervasive in all Christian scripture. And through the twenty centuries of Christian history, it is a point to which Christian theologians and ethicists have returned again and again. In the great tradition of Christian moral thought, it is a very dangerous thing to be wealthy. It is at least the most urgent obligation of the affluent to care for those in need.

Given the breadth and systemic character of poverty, it seems clear that our search for solutions must again return to institutional structures. Acts of charity by individuals and churches, laudable as they often are, are no substitute in amount or scope for public commitment. Room exists for a good deal of debate over the particulars; there should be no question about the need to make the commitment.

So this book should help with the ongoing dialog, especially among Christians. I'd like to see it studied in churches throughout the land.

One thing more, on a more personal level. I have recently left my academic post as a Christian ethicist to become a pastor of a large church in the center of Washington, D.C. Here the issues of poverty are not at all academic. We are surrounded here by people in need, and our community of faith contains numbers of people in the worlds of business and government and education who want to struggle more with the issues addressed in the book. So I am especially grateful for the chapters on preaching. Everybody who enjoys the privilege of preaching has a special responsibility to make the pulpit ring with concern for poor people. I trust that many preachers will be stimulated by these pages to go beyond what they read here in making their own unique contributions to Christian thought and action.

J. PHILIP WOGAMAN
Senior Minister, Foundry United Methodist Church

NOTE

1. Gilder, George, *Wealth and Poverty* (New York: Basic Books, 1981), 118.

Acknowledgments

I am delighted to thank the persons who have made this book possible. Elmhurst College has been wonderfully supportive of the Niebuhr Conference and of *Standing with the Poor*. The president, Ivan E. Frick, and the academic dean, John E. Bohnert, have taken personal interest in the projects and have committed the resources of the institution to them. Without their active support neither the conference nor the book would have come about. The Department of Theology could not have been more encouraging, especially during the transition from one chairperson—professor Armin Limper has retired after more than a generation of service to the college—to another, Ron Goetz. The grace of these two senior professors far exceeds my unalterable affection for them. The Elmhurst College administration and my department have allowed me the freedom and granted the resources to do the work that theologians must be about in church-related colleges. Lastly, I appreciate the patience and guidance of the folks at The Pilgrim Press. Their kind encouragement and wise counsel have always been on target.

Introduction

Paul Plenge Parker

When I first read the works of Martin Luther King, Jr., I "heard" them as if they were from the Bible. They were true, they were important, and they applied to me. His sermons made the Scriptures relevant to the needs of the world. Intractable social problems became soluble—if only we would try to solve them.

Through King, I heard the word of God. God's way of doing things excluded no one. God's way included all persons and all things because the universe was one huge tapestry woven with the complementary threads of love and justice. King preached that love was "the great unifying force of life."[1] This reconciliation of all things was God's original purpose, according to Paul's letter to the Ephesians. To King, love was the only means consistent with God's goal and therefore the only means that could overcome this country's three great evils—poverty, racism, and violence.

King's understanding of the interconnectedness of human existence and of these three great moral threats has guided the formation of this volume. All of the contributing writers have taken it as axiomatic that poverty has shredded the fabric of humanity. They have come together in an interdisciplinary effort to struggle against poverty, knowing that inevitably they would also confront racism and violence—often experienced as sexism. They hope that their work will bear the fruit of reconciliation in the church and across the country.

Just as Martin Luther King has influenced the content of this book, the Niebuhr brothers have figured significantly into its texture. Reinhold Niebuhr understood the limits and the tragedy of human existence. His analysis could find the soft underbelly of any institution, system of thought, or human claim to finality. The analytical essays of this book follow in this tradition.

The enduring influence of H. Richard Niebuhr is also visible. Each chapter reflects Richard's conviction that our central loyalty and every response belong to God. For many persons his dictum has come to be taken for granted: "God is acting in all actions on you. So respond to all actions upon you as to respond to his action." From this fundamental belief, imbued with Richard's grasp of the social nature of existence, poverty can be understood to be a horrible human condition through which God acts on each individual and the entire community. So in your work against poverty, respond to God.[2]

Beyond the pervasive significance of the Niebuhrs for American theology, their influence is manifest in these pages because all of the writers were leaders at the 1990 Niebuhr Conference on the Church and Society. The annual conference is sponsored by Elmhurst College primarily for the church but also for the broader society. The college hopes that the conference can function as a catalyst for change in America. It is intended for Christians who are committed to engaging the scourges of poverty, racism, and violence through critical analyses and as a response of deepest loyalty to God. Like *Standing with the Poor*, each year the conference focuses on one of the three great national evils through social scientific analyses, theological analyses, and practical ministerial applications. The authors of this volume, while addressing the social sins that King identified, wrote under the influence of the Niebuhrs.

Standing with the Poor has three related sections. The first part is a social scientific assessment of poverty and welfare. Drawing from his work with the Panel Study of Income Dynamics, economist Greg Duncan focuses the first two chapters on childhood poverty, its causes, and its likely remedies. Most of us are shocked that 20 percent of America's children, half of whom are African-American, live in poverty. Yet the panel's twenty-five-year longitudinal research shows that poverty is actually more broadly experienced and cuts deeper into the African-American community. Thirty-three percent of America's children have lived in poverty during at least one year of their childhood, about 12 percent have lived in poverty between five and ten years of their childhood, and fewer than one Black child in seven lives comfortably above the poverty threshold. Duncan, writing as a social scientist, not a Christian ethicist, laments that this is unjustified.

Like a fresh breeze, Duncan's research blows away the social ignorance that often hides poverty's causes and the church's opportunities. The conditions that lead to childhood poverty, all of which are adult problems, are surprisingly clear, discrete, and correctable. Many persons have sensed them all along, despite misleading cultural platitudes. The causes include (1) increasing income inequality; (2) stagnant or falling wages relative to inflation; (3) loss of employment; (4) a dramatic increase of single-parent families due to divorce and out-of-wedlock births; and (5) a "real" decline in cash transfer benefits.

At the conclusion of his first essay and throughout the second, Duncan offers a number of public policies that could respond effectively to the causes of childhood poverty: (1) transfer benefits regardless of the causes that give rise to the parents' need; (2) greater investments in the future of children through programs such as Head Start and WIC; (3) supplements to low wages and increases in the minimum wage; (4) job-training programs; and (5) more rigorous judicial enforcement of child-support payments from noncustodial divorced parents. Finally, says Duncan, concern for the possibility of parental welfare dependence must be counterbalanced by the certainty of the detrimental effects of poverty on children.

Though Duncan does not highlight the church's responsibilities in this age of heightened inequality (as an economist he has no obligation here), many are immediately apparent. His economic research, for instance, cries out for churches to emphasize once again the crucial necessity of both a socially responsible ethic and a high personal morality. Because every Sunday school teacher emphasizes the importance of sharing, it is reasonable to expect pastors to teach about the virtue of national sharing. The point of sharing, whether individually or socially through public transfer benefits, is to help those in need—widows, sojourners, and orphans: the elderly, the unemployed, and children— those who are expected to make it on their own without the requisite social skills. St. Paul admonished the Corinthians to share to the point of economic equality (2 Cor. 8), and we teach our children to "cut the cake into equal slices," so it surely is not too much to expect that sermons address economic equality.

Working from Duncan's research, sermons can now return to a high personal sexual ethic without fear of being labeled prudish or dangerously repressive. It is not only good Christian morality, it is also good economics. In light of the catastrophic rate of divorce and out-of-wedlock births, sermons on divorce, marital fidelity, and premarital sexual relationships need to be preached on Sunday mornings in addition to the more typical small, sexually segregated study groups. Sadly, too, as a mark of the church's full participation in the American ethos, pastors must now teach church members who are noncustodial parents that they have a moral responsibility to pay child support.

The situations traditionally regarded as social and the problems typically viewed as personal need to be addressed from the pulpit if the richness of God's Reign is to replace the poverty of the world. We need to find gracious words to address demanding issues so that God's Reign can "come on earth as it is in heaven." It is part of the good news for our society and for our children.

The second section of this book is a theological and ethical examination of poverty and the grounds for serving the poor. Jacquelyn Grant observes that victims of poverty in America are disproportionately Black and female, even after accounting for some of the most powerful variables that lead to poverty. Worse than the physical deprivation is the spiritual agony and social degradation that women and African-Americans suffer as their dignity is assaulted. When churches do not visibly resist the forces of poverty, racism, and sexism (within the church itself even more than in society), they publicly, though perhaps only implicitly, approve of a white racist and patriarchal concept of God that alienates women, African-Americans, and many spiritually sensitive persons. Those whose freedom is most significantly limited are kept the greatest distance from the God of freedom.

Ronald Goetz, a self-confessed bleeding-heart liberal who has identified with nearly every liberationist movement that has come along, and usually before it was popular, offers a friendly but biting critique of such groups. All American liberationists have imbibed from the common cultural wells of progressive individualism and utilitarian pragmatism, says Goetz. In effect, the liberationist movements serve their own self-interests by whatever means they perceive to be most effective, despite the common result that they ultimately betray their own movement as well as others. Goetz sees Christian liberation as something different: inclusive justice, mercy, and responsibility in one's personal relationships and the social context.

Avoiding Goetz's criticism and answering Grant's cry of dereliction, James Cone lays out the necessary theological presuppositions for an adequate theology of liberation. The Bible plays several critical roles. The Scriptures are the primary source of theology's central paradigms: the Exodus, the universalization of freedom in Jesus, and the power of liberation in his crucifixion and resurrection. The Bible also functions as an external critic to liberation movements, calling for greater loyalty to the Reign of God than to the dominant culture. Cone ends with the principle that the truth of theology "is found in whether the people receive the extra strength to fight until freedom comes."

How can ministers test and then preach their theological convictions about poverty? The third section of *Standing with the Poor* attempts to answer this question in two ways. First, David Buttrick offers a biblically informed, insightful, and superbly helpful analysis of the American pulpit's social bondage. He then extracts from the Black church tradition four features of a biblical liberation hermeneutic that can help preachers free themselves from cultural captivation. This is a crucial essay for every minister who hopes to interpret the Scriptures faithfully.

The last four chapters are sermons on the problem of poverty. Through the story of King Ahab and Naboth, Wallace Smith focuses on the requirements of truth and integrity for all persons, whether national leaders or average citizens. Though perhaps momentarily frustrated, God's universal justice will ultimately reign. Gail O'Day works from the prophet Joel and the parable of Lazarus to remind us that God still stands against the rich and with the poor—and so must the church. June Yoder offers an intimate seed for a sermon. After all of our struggles to be faithful, we, sadly, still want a gospel that is less challenging. We finally do not want to follow Jesus to the cross. Jorge Morales preaches from a classic text of ecclesiastic discrimination and protest. He draws out a theological rationale for political action that ends discrimination, empowers the underclass, builds the church, and advances the Reign of God. He finds that the church is an institution like all others, yet called to be different—to accept those unlike itself, to receive the immigrant, the poor, the unpopular, the outcast.

NOTES

1. Martin Luther King, Jr., *Strength to Love* (Philadelphia: Fortress Press, 1963), 145.
2. H. Richard Niebuhr, *The Responsible Self* (New York: Harper & Row, 1963), 126.

I

Economic Analyses of Poverty and Welfare

Chicago: World Class City, etching

1

Economic Poverty—
Causes and Effects

Greg J. Duncan

1. INTRODUCTION

Poverty continues to plague many Americans, despite an unprecedented level of material wealth produced by economic growth. Using a yardstick that compares income with a poverty threshold set at about $12,000 for a family of four, the U.S. Census Bureau in 1988 counted 32 million poor people in the country, about 40 percent of whom were children and about half of whom were Black or Hispanic.[1]

This chapter summarizes important features of economic poverty in the United States, with particular emphasis on families with children. More than 3 million of the country's poor in 1988 were elderly, and while we do not mean to minimize their economic problems, we shall see that the incidence of poverty has lessened substantially for the elderly over the past several decades. In contrast, poverty among children was just as prevalent in the late 1980s as it had been two decades before.

We begin with an examination of trends in poverty among children and the elderly in the United States. About one in five children in this country in the 1980s was poor, a rate that was much higher than in other advanced Western countries. Although varying widely across ethnic groups, poverty rates for each group were higher than estimated in either the 1970 or the 1980 census, although lower than in 1950 or 1960. The dramatic increase in the prevalence of single-parent families,

3

a sluggish labor market, and declining benefit levels in transfer programs all played a role in the increased prevalence of poverty.

The rates show the percentages of children in the midst of periods of poverty when the survey "snapshot" was taken, but provide no direct information on the dynamic aspects of poverty among children. Section 3 examines the prevalence of poverty over the entire period of childhood and finds that much childhood poverty is short-lived, although long-term poverty, especially among Black children, is by no means unimportant.

Apart from the average level of economic resources during childhood, another critical variable of economic status is income volatility. Research on sharp income drops during the Great Depression and more recent periods has found long-lasting adverse effects on individuals' mental and physical health. Section 4 reviews the evidence on the prevalence of income volatility and its links to important life events such as divorce or unemployment.

Evidence on the effect of parental income on children's life chances is reviewed in section 5. The few studies that have measured both parental income and other background characteristics typically have found important income effects, even after adjusting for the effects of other characteristics. Some policy implications are presented in Section 6.

2. INCIDENCE OF POVERTY ACROSS TIME AND NATIONS

Despite its prosperous economy, the United States in 1979 was almost unique among advanced Western nations in the high fraction of its citizens living in poverty (12 percent; Table 1, column 1).[2] Indeed, the only country with a similar rate included in the comparisons was Great Britain, which had a per capita national income only two-thirds that of the United States. Although the overall rate of poverty in the United States is lower now than in 1959, there has been no discernible downward trend in the overall incidence of poverty since in the late 1960s.

U.S. trends are much more dramatic if the fortunes of the elderly and children are tracked separately (Table 1, columns 2 and 3). Poverty rates among the elderly in this country have fallen steadily during the post–World War II period. Many fewer of the elderly are poor in the United States than in Great Britain, while roughly equal fractions of the

Table 1

Percentage of Persons Poor in Various Countries

	All persons (%)	Elderly (%)	Children (%)
United States			
1988	13	12	20
1979	12	15	16
1969	12	25	14
1959	22	35	27
Canada, 1981	7	8	10
Germany, 1981	8	15	8
Great Britain, 1970	12	37	11

Source: Smeeding (1988).

Note: In 1984, per capita income (in U.S. dollars) was $15,700 in the United States, $14,330 in Canada, $11,500 in Germany, and $10,255 in Great Britain.

elderly are poor in the U.S. and Germany. By both historical and international standards, many of the elderly in the United States by the 1990s enjoyed reasonably comfortable standards of living.

In contrast, the economic position of many children in the country is worse than it was two decades ago. In 1988, one in five children in the United States lived in families with incomes below the poverty threshold, a rate that was twice that of Canada, Germany, and Great Britain around 1980, the most recent time for which data are available.

A longer view shows that the period since the end of World War II has seen remarkable economic growth and concomitant reductions in the fraction of children living in households with incomes below the poverty line. In 1949, one of every two children was poor; for Black children the rate was seven of eight (Table 2, rows 1 and 3). Poverty rates for all ethnic groups fell by about twenty percentage points between 1949 and 1959 and by ten to twenty percentage points during the 1960s. Poverty rates have generally risen since the early 1970s, rising during recessions and falling only moderately or holding steady during periods of economic expansion. By the mid-1980s, after several years of recovery from the severe recession of 1981–82, childhood pov-

Table 2

Poverty Rates for Children across Time by Ethnic Group

	1949 (%)	1959 (%)	1969 (%)	1979 (%)	1985 (%)
All children	48	26	16	17	20
White, not Hispanic	41	19	10	12	13
Black, not Hispanic	87	63	41	36	41
Hispanic	73	53	33	28	37

Source: Danziger (1989b), based on data from the 1950, 1960, 1970, and 1980 dicennial censuses and the 1986 Current Population Survey.
Note: For 1949–79, children 0–14; for 1985, children 0–18.

erty was still more prevalent than at the time of the 1970 census.

What accounts for the frustrating increase in childhood poverty during the 1970s and 1980s? Many culprits have been suggested, including a sluggish macroeconomic environment that lowered the real incomes of families in all economic strata, greater inequality in the distribution of income, increasing numbers of families headed by women, stagnant wages for young workers, decreases unrelated to business cycles in the labor-force involvement of men, especially minority men, and a decline in the value of transfer benefits available to low-income families. In varying degrees, almost all of these played a role.

Assembled in Table 3 is evidence on trends in a number of these factors as they relate to poverty among families with children.[3] Data are presented for three years—1970, 1978, and 1986—that span the period of research and avoid times of unusually good or bad economic conditions. The rate of poverty for families with children rose during this period by an average of about one percentage point every four years (from 11 to 15 percent in sixteen years; Table 3, row 1), with much of the growth occurring during the recessions of the mid-1970s and early 1980s and the sharp inflation of the late 1970s. In contrast to earlier periods, the times of economic expansion, especially during the 1980s,

Table 3

Characteristics of Families with Children, 1970–86

		1970	1978	1986
		(by %, unless indicated)		
1.	Poverty rate for families with children[a]	11	12	15
	Increasing income inequality Change in "adjusted" family income for families with children, relative to 1970			
2.	Median families[b]	100	113	114
3.	Poorest 20% of families[b]	100	103	88
4.	Richest 20% of families[b]	100	116	127
5.	Head under age 25[c]	100	100	82
	Family structure			
6.	Families with children headed by single mothers[d]	11	17	20
	Poverty rate for families with children			
7.	Married couple[a]	6	5	7
8.	Single mothers[a]	45	41	46
9.	Poverty rate for families with children if families had 1970 composition patterns[e]	11	12	12
	Labor market Median earnings of full-year, full-time male workers (in thousands of 1986 dollars)[f]			
10.	Age 20–24	$17.5	$16.7	$14.2
11.	Age 25–34	$24.0	$25.8	$22.7
	Families in bottom 20% of income distribution with one or more full-time workers[g]			
12.	All families	38	29	24
13.	Families with both parents[g]	58	55	54
14.	Families with single mothers[g]	5	3	3
	Cash transfers Average cash transfers received by pre-transfer poor (in thousands of 1984 dollars)[h]			
15.	Married couples	$4.0	$3.8	$2.9
16.	Single mothers	$5.2	$4.1	$3.3

[a]CBO (1988), Table C-2. Poverty thresholds are adjusted with the CPI-X1 price index.
[b]CBO (1988), Table A-4. Adjustments to family income are made for family size and inflation as measured by the CPI-X1 price index.
[c]CBO (1988), Table A-10.
[d]CBO (1988), Table A-1.
[e]Calculations by the author based on CBO (1988).
[f]U.S. Bureau of the Census, Current Population Reports, Series P-60, various issues, adjusted with the CPI-X1 price index.
[g]CBO (1988), Table A-12.
[h]Danzinger and Gottschalk (1985). Figures in the "1970" column are for 1973, figures in the "1978" column are for 1979, and figures in the "1986" column are for 1984. Dollar amounts have been adjusted by the conventional Consumer Price Index.

were not of sufficient benefit to low-income families to allow the poverty rates to retreat to their pre-recession levels.

Income inequality. At the heart of the phenomenon of increasing childhood poverty is the striking contrast between the changing economic fortunes of families at the top, middle, and bottom of the income distribution since the beginning of the 1970s. Income inequality increased sharply over the period of research, reversing a modest egalitarian trend that had prevailed since the end of World War II (Danziger and Gottschalk, 1985; Phillips, 1990). The increasing inequality more than offset modest improvements in average living standards, producing an increase in childhood poverty.

Families with the median income distribution enjoyed a modest improvement in their economic status. When, as in Table 3, family incomes are adjusted for family size and an inflation index that treats housing costs in a more reasonable way than the conventional Consumer Price Index is used, the resulting increase in the economic well-being of families at the middle of the distribution is about 14 percent between 1970 and 1986 (Table 3, row 2).

Had the distribution of income remained unchanged, we would have observed an identical fourteen percentage point income increase for families at the top and bottom of the income distribution. Instead, families in the bottom fifth of the 1986 income distribution had adjusted incomes that were only 88 percent of what they had received in 1970 (row 3). Families in the top fifth enjoyed living standards that were 27 percent higher in 1986 than 1970 (row 4). Thus, incomes for families with children became much less equally distributed over this period.

An increasingly unequal income distribution produced more childhood poverty in 1986 than in 1970, despite a general increase in living standards.

This rules out one item from our list of suspected culprits—a disastrous economic environment shared by families at all income levels—and shifts the emphasis to factors that caused families at the bottom of the distribution to fall even further behind other families.

Family structure. Roughly twice as many families with children were headed by women in 1986 than 1970 (20 percent versus 11 percent; Table 3, row 6), and the incidence of poverty among female-headed families has consistently been seven to eight times higher than among married-couple families (rows 7 and 8). These two factors combined to account for virtually all of the increased prevalence of poverty among families with children and to shift the majority of poor families from the "married couple" category to the "single mothers" category. Had the survey of families in 1986 shown the same proportions of married-couple families and mother-only families that had prevailed in 1970, the 1986 poverty rate would have been 12 percent rather than 15 percent (rows 1 and 9). In contrast, similar calculations show no role for familial structural change in childhood poverty for the decade between 1950 and 1960 and a very modest role between 1960 and 1970.

Labor-market conditions. There is little doubt that the economic growth of the 1950s and 1960s was primarily responsible for the large drops in poverty during that time. Nor is there any doubt that the business cycles of the 1970s and 1980s, especially the recessions in the mid-1970s and early 1980s, produced corresponding changes in the prevalence of poverty. However, the labor market of the 1970s and 1980s was shaped by a number of massive and seemingly contradictory changes. Despite the severe recessions, the economy employed some 30 million more workers in 1986 than in 1970, enabling large numbers of baby-boomers and women of all ages to find work. At the same time, however, unemployment increased substantially and the earnings of those finding work often failed to keep pace with inflation.

The disappointing earning trends were not limited to the more marginal members of the labor force. Shown in Table 3, rows 10 and 11, are earnings of full-time, full-year male workers. Inflation-adjusted earnings of twenty- to twenty-four-year-old and twenty-five- to thirty-four-year-old men were higher in 1970 than they were sixteen years later in 1986, a situation that was without precedent in the post-war period (Levy, 1986). Earnings for other workers generally fared as badly, making it increasingly difficult for low-wage workers to earn their way out of poverty.

Despite the employment boom, certain subgroups of working-age individuals, especially minority men, were much less attached to the labor market in 1986 than in 1970. As shown in Table 3, rows 12 to 14, families with children in the bottom 20 percent of the income distribution were much less likely to have one or more full-time earners in 1986 than in 1970. Part of this trend could be attributed to the increased prevalence of low-income female-headed families, for whom labor force participation rates were exceedingly low. Taken together, sluggish wages and falling labor force attachment reduced the importance of income from the labor market in the income packages of low-income families with children and brought more of them into poverty.

Transfers.   Cash benefits paid by the programs most likely to benefit families with children—in particular Aid to Families with Dependent Children (AFDC)—generally lost ground to inflation during this period (Table 3, rows 15 and 16). In 1986 dollars, the median state paid nearly $600 per month to a qualifying AFDC family of four in 1970 and $400 per month in 1986—a loss of 33 percent. Gottschalk and Danziger (1985) estimate that transfer income changes were about as important as labor-market changes in accounting for changes in the overall poverty rate between 1967 and 1979. Noncash transfers, in particular Medicaid, fared much better during this period, making the total effect of trends in transfers on childhood poverty considerably more benign than implied by Table 3.

The United States' relatively low cash transfer programs benefit levels go a long way toward explaining why the poverty rate for children is so much higher in this country than in other Western countries. Compared to other industrialized countries, the United States clearly spends less on transfers per poor family with children, brings fewer such families out of poverty with those transfers, and has more holes in its safety net than almost any other country (Smeeding, 1988).

In sum, the rising poverty rate for children during the 1970s and 1980s was the product of a number of factors. Despite a modest increase in the living standards of the median family, growing family income inequality—fueled by stagnant wages for young workers, increasing numbers of families headed by women, reduced labor-force attachment of prime-age, especially minority, men, and falling transfer program benefit levels—pushed increasing numbers of children into poverty.

Trends in the concentration of urban poverty.   One final and also troubling recent trend is an increased geographic concentration of the urban poor between 1970 and 1980. Although not focused solely on children, the figures in Table 4 show that substantially higher numbers of Black poor lived in neighborhoods in which many of their neighbors were also poor. In 1980, only 8 percent of the poor whites lived in census tracts with a poverty rate of 40 percent or higher, but 36 percent of the poor Blacks lived in census tracts characterized by a rate of poverty equal to or greater than 40 percent. If the resulting social isolation of poor children raised in high-poverty neighborhoods is detrimental to their life chances, as Wilson (1987) and others believe, then the trend is particularly troubling.[4]

3. PATTERNS OF FIFTEEN-YEAR CHILDHOOD POVERTY

The Census Bureau's periodic "snapshots" of the rates of poverty show the extent of childhood poverty at the time they are taken. They fail, however, to state the situation unambiguously and to measure the persistence of poverty across an individual's childhood. Finding that one-fifth of all children are poor in each of five consecutive years, for example, is consistent with two very different scenarios: one of high turnover, in which all children were poor in only one year, and another of great persistence, in which the same children were poor all five years and the remaining 80 percent of children experienced no poverty at all.

Duncan and Rodgers (1988) use data from the Panel Study of Income Dynamics to analyze fifteen-year poverty patterns of children who were under the age of four in 1968, the first year of the study, and for whom data covering the family economic conditions of their childhoods for fifteen years are available (Table 5). They distinguish six categories of economic status: family income below the poverty level for (1) one to four, (2) five to nine, (3) ten to fourteen, or (4) all fifteen years; (5) family income never below the poverty level but below 150 percent of it for at least one year; and (6) family income always at least 150 percent of

Table 4

Distribution of Poor Whites and Poor Blacks
Living in the Fifty Largest Central Cities by Poverty Rate
in the Census Tract of Residence, 1970 and 1980

Percentage in poverty in the census tract	Poor whites		Poor Blacks	
	1970 (%)	1980 (%)	1970 (%)	1980 (%)
Under 20%	64	66	20	16
20–29%	18	17	26	21
30–39%	10	9	27	27
40% and over	8	8	27	36

Source: Ellwood (1988), based on data from the 1970 and 1980 censuses.

the poverty level.

Duncan and Rodgers (1988) find that many more children come into contact with poverty than experience persistent poverty (Table 5). While one-third of all children experience poverty in at least one year, only about one child in twenty experiences poverty over ten or more years of his or her childhood. However, persistent childhood poverty is far from insignificant, since an estimated 4.8 percent of all children experience poverty during at least two-thirds of their childhood years, and an additional 7 percent are poor for between five and nine of the fifteen years.

Within these patterns of persistent childhood poverty Bane and Ellwood also find a striking racial distinction. As shown in Table 5, fewer than one in seven Black children lived comfortably above the poverty line throughout the fifteen-year period and more than one-quarter were poor for at least ten of the fifteen years. Blacks accounted for nearly 90 percent of the children who were poor during at least ten out of fifteen years.

Table 6 contains Duncan and Rodgers's 1988 estimation of the prevalence of childhood poverty for various subgroups in the population. Many household characteristics have substantial effects on the estimated prevalence of poverty, effects that often differ by race. Disability has the most powerful and consistent effects across both racial sub-

Table 5
Fifteen-Year Poverty Experiences of Children Under the Age of Four in 1968 by Race

| | Always above 150% of poverty line (%) | Distribution of poverty categories within racial groups (rows add to 100%) | | | | | | Mean number of years poor (%) | Unweighted number of observations |
		Never poor, but not always above 150% of poverty line (%)	Poor 1–4 years (%)	Poor 5–9 years (%)	Poor 10–14 years (%)	Poor 15 years (%)	All (%)		
Non-Black	55.7	19.3	19.8	4.6	0.6	0.0	100.0%	0.9	531
Black	13.0	8.0	32.3	17.7	24.0	4.9	100.0%	5.5	493
All	48.4	17.7	22.1	7.0	4.1	0.7	100.0%	1.5	1075

Source: Duncan and Rodgers (1988), based on data from the Panel Study of Income Dynamics.

groups. Black children living in families where the household head was disabled during the entire fifteen-year period could expect to be poor in almost eleven of the fifteen years; the comparable figure for whites was 3.3 years.

Several of the measures of family structure have powerful effects on the expected amount of childhood poverty. The largest differential effect for the two racial subgroups is linked with the marital status of the mother at the time of a child's birth. White children who are born to never-married mothers, a relatively small group, can expect to spend more than one-third of their first fifteen years in poverty—a figure that is considerably higher than any other in Table 6 for whites and the only one that is as high for whites as for Blacks. For Blacks, birth to a never-married mother increases the expected prevalence of poverty only slightly—from 5.4 to 6.0 of the first fifteen years of childhood.

In general, patterns of family structure are powerful determinants of the economic fates of both white and Black children. Living with one rather than two parents throughout childhood increases the expected years of childhood poverty for white children from 0.5 to 3.2 years. The comparable increase for Blacks is relatively smaller—from 3.0 to 7.3 years—but larger than that for whites in absolute terms. These figures reveal the surprising fact that the expected prevalence of poverty among Black children living in continuously two-parent families is about as high as that for white children who spend their entire childhood in single-parent families. Family structure differences between Black and white families are obviously not the sole reason for the discrepancy between the amounts of poverty experienced by the two groups of children.

Locational measures have stronger effects for Blacks than for whites, with a much higher prevalence of poverty among Blacks in rural and southern areas and a considerably lower prevalence in large urban areas. Apart from disability of the household head, rural location is the most powerful factor associated with Black childhood poverty.

The final characteristic examined, the education level of the household head, has surprisingly modest effects on the prevalence of childhood poverty, especially for Blacks. Even when their head of the household is a high-school graduate, Black children can expect to spend more than five of their first fifteen years below the poverty line.

Table 6
Expected Years of Childhood Poverty out of Fifteen
Associated with Various Household Characteristics

| | Expected years of poverty | |
	White and other	Black
All households	0.8	5.4
Household at birth of child		
Never-married mother	6.2	6.0
Teenaged mother	1.2	5.4
Education of head		
8 years	1.2	5.6
12 years	0.7	5.3
Household during all of childhood[a]		
Head disabled	3.3	10.9
Lives in South	0.8	6.4
Lives out of South	0.7	4.3
Lives in large city	0.7	3.9
Lives in rural area	1.1	8.1
Lives with 1 parent	3.2	7.3
Lives with 2 parents	0.5	3.0

Source: Duncan and Rodgers (1988), based on data from the Panel Study of Income Dynamics.
[a]The expected years are estimated from the proportion of children in households with the specified characteristic who were born in poverty and from the observed transition probabilities for children in such households.

4. INCOME VOLATILITY

The mixture of transitory and persistent poverty for children shown in Table 5 suggests that family incomes exhibit substantial instability. This is important because a growing body of evidence suggests that sharp losses of income, even if they do not reduce income to below-poverty levels, may produce long-lasting effects on the mental and possibly physical health of the adults experiencing them. Apart from parenting behavior, we know virtually nothing about corresponding effects on children.

The most extensive studies of the long-term consequences of income loss were conducted by Elder and Liker and their colleagues, who used longitudinal data collected over several decades from a sample of Berkeley-area married couples with children to perform a series of sophisticated analyses.[5]

Couples experiencing a drop of one-third or more in family income between 1929 and the early 1930s were compared on a range of subsequent outcomes—marital and parent-child relationships and mental and physical health—with couples whose depression-era incomes did not fall as much. Some of the outcomes were measured several decades later.

The researchers found that for men, the income losses produced uniformly harmful effects on marital and parenting behavior, apparently not so much because of the loss of income as because of the stress caused by the loss of status as breadwinner. Women from less advantaged families also experienced harmful effects on their marriages, parenting behavior, and subsequent health. For these working-class women, the income loss itself appeared to be the culprit; they were left with too few resources to perform properly their functions as homemakers. Interestingly, women from middle-class backgrounds who experienced income losses subsequently did better than did otherwise similar women who escaped such adversity. Their resources for coping were apparently adequate, and the economic hardship actually made them better able to handle subsequent problems.

Dramatic income losses were found to have diverse effects on children. In general, these effects were more detrimental for boys than for girls and when they resulted from income losses occurring early in childhood as opposed to during the adolescent years. Ties between fathers and sons suffered the most; ties between mothers and daughters appeared to be strengthened by the economic losses. Virtually none of these effects persisted very far into the adult years.

The prevalence of dramatic drops in living standards during the 1969 to 1979 period was analyzed by Duncan (1988) and Burkhauser and Duncan (1988a). Their measure of income volatility consisted of instances in which living standards fell by more than 50 percent in consecutive years. The first column of Table 7 shows that the risk of this occurrence was substantial: more than one-quarter of white children and one-third of Black children were estimated to have experienced such a drop at least once during the eleven-year period. Nearly all of these decreases left the families with modest incomes at best. Compounding the potential problems caused by these losses was the fact that the families containing children were much less likely than other families to have predicted the losses before they occurred and to have had savings available to cope with their financial consequences. Savings cushions were especially unlikely in Black families with children.

An examination of the links between the events and the incidence of major income losses showed that divorce or separation was the most important family composition event associated with an income-to-needs drop and could be linked to one-seventh of the losses for white children and one-fifth of the losses for Black children. A major period of unemployment was the most frequent labor-market change, followed by reductions in labor supply due to illness of the family head (Duncan, 1988).

5. DOES INCOME MATTER?

There can be little doubt that the average child raised in a poor household has a less enjoyable childhood than the typical child raised in greater affluence. Poverty standards reflect society's judgments of minimally acceptable living standards. Because children are completely dependent upon others for their security and can in no way be held responsible for their economic situation, there is a sense that allowing them to live in households with living standards below the poverty line, especially persistently, is socially unjustified.

Somewhat less clear-cut is the extent to which poverty, especially persistent poverty, reduces the opportunities for success during adulthood. This section reviews the evidence on this point, with an eye toward distinguishing the effects of poverty from other characteristics of poor families and the environments in which they live.

Most work on the effects of family background on child development lacks explicit poverty measures and effectively equates family

Table 7
Various Indicators of Income Volatility
for Children and Individuals of All Ages

Age and race in 1969	Percent with family income/needs falling by more than 50% at least once, 1969–79	Of those with income/needs falling by more than 50%	
		Percent living in families expecting the loss	Percent living in families with substantial savings prior to loss
Individuals less than 5 years old			
All	27	6	42
White	26	7	48
Black	35	4	16
Individuals of all ages	31	14	56

Source: Duncan (1988a), based on data from the Panel Study of Income Dynamics.
Note: Income/needs is the ratio of family income to a poverty threshold based on family size.

background with social class. Class is usually measured by some combination of the occupational and educational attainments of the parents. This view of family background is implicitly based on the notion that one's social class is fixed at birth and does not change throughout childhood.

However permanent social class may seem, our review of the evidence on the economic resources available throughout childhood shows these resources to be quite volatile. Many more children experience temporary poverty than persistent poverty. Events such as unemployment and divorce produce dramatic changes in living standards at all levels of the income distribution.

Indeed, given the extent of some of the changes, it is hard to imagine that the perception and reality of social class could fail to change as well. Divorce often moves middle-class women and children into a working-class environment, or working-class women and children into poverty, if at times only temporarily.

Since social policy can affect family income more easily than almost any other family characteristic, it is important for public-policymakers to discover how changes in family income during childhood might be expected to affect the life chances of children. One can imagine an experiment in which the incomes of randomly chosen families are either permanently augmented or "shocked" with sharp increases so that the long-term success of children raised in those families can be compared with that of children in otherwise similar families with lower or stable incomes. The Negative Income Tax experiments approximated these conditions for income augmentation, and an examination of their effects on children often showed beneficial results (Salkind and Haskins, 1982). Certain subsets of children in families in the experimental higher-income group had greater increases in reading scores, lower dropout rates, and better diets than did control group children.

Nonexperimental studies of the effects of parental income have been forced to use observations of "natural" experiments of children who have been raised in families with different income levels and trajectories. Researchers have then had to rely on statistical controls to adjust for the many other ways in which life in a high-income family confers advantages.

Hill et al. (1985, Table D. 1) compared the relative success of children raised in the bottom and top quintiles of the income distribution. They found that while only a minority (43.4 percent) of the children raised in families in the bottom fifth ended up in the bottom fifth as young adults, that fraction was far greater than the comparable fraction (9.2 percent) of children raised in the most affluent fifth of parental families who ended up in the bottom fifth as adults. Only one in fifty (2.2 percent) of the children raised in families in the lowest income quintile had reached the highest quintile, as compared with more than one in three (35.9 percent) children raised in families in the highest fifth.

Although reduced in size, the effects of parental income on the success of children persist even after researchers have controlled for differences in the more conventional measures of parental background, such as the education levels and occupational prestige of the parents.

Sewell and Hauser (1975) analyzed a sample of Wisconsin high-school graduates and found highly significant effects of the taxable income of parents on the completed schooling and particularly on the earnings of sons at about age twenty-five. They concluded: "There can be little doubt that the association of socioeconomic background variables with son's earnings is due solely to the intergenerational effect of parents' income, while the latter cannot to any large extent be explained by differing abilities, educational attainments, or occupational achievements of the sons of rich and poor families" (p. 84).

Studies based on national samples from the National Longitudinal Surveys (e.g., Shaw, 1982) and the PSID (e.g., McLanahan, 1985; Hill and Duncan, 1987) that include measures of both parental income and other social background factors also find a significant role for income in the attainments of children.

The few studies that focus on the effects of poverty experiences during childhood on adult attainments also find significant effects, especially if poverty has persisted for a number of years. Corcoran et al. (1987) controlled for an elaborate set of social background and family structure measures and still found highly significant and substantively large, detrimental effects of the persistence of poverty during childhood on the later earnings and family incomes of sons. To our knowledge, no studies have systematically examined the links between income volatility during childhood and later attainments.

At this point, the highly suggestive links between the persistence of poverty during childhood and adult attainments can only be described as a black box. Subjecting a child to poverty during a substantial period of childhood lowers the odds that the child will have a successful career as a adult. Adjustments for measurable characteristics associated with persistent poverty (e.g., living with a single parent, less-educated parents, or parents with less prestigious jobs, or living in a "bad" neighborhood) do not explain away poverty's detrimental effect. Little is known about the mechanisms involved, however, and as argued in the subsequent section, much more needs to be learned before we can point with confidence to a set of policies that will break the suspected link between persistent poverty and later achievement.

6. POLICY ISSUES

In 1988 some 12.6 million children lived in families with incomes below the poverty line. It would have taken about $19 billion in that year to eliminate poverty among children, i.e., to give all poor families with children incomes equal to the poverty line (Committee on Ways and Means, 1990). The comparable gap for the nation's 3.5 million elderly poor was $3 billion. The $19 billion "poverty gap" for children is about as large as the cash assistance currently paid by Aid to Families with Dependent Children, but only about one-tenth as large as the total cost of Social Security retirement cash benefits. Would the problems of poverty among children be eliminated if the country were able to summon the political will necessary to eliminate the poverty gap?

The answer to this question depends on the research issues discussed above: To what extent is income itself responsible for affecting the life chances of children? If income does matter, what are the mechanisms involved? Are the adverse effects of income loss the result of the changed living standard or of other aspects of the event that produced the loss?

Presuming that income itself matters, there are a set of complementary ways in which policies can be directed at children at risk. One way is through income transfers to poor families with children. Transfer programs such as food stamps or Aid to Families with Dependent Children make their benefits conditional on low income itself, regardless of the reason that income came to be low. Other transfers (e.g., unemployment compensation, child support) are directed at income losses associated with the events that caused the losses.

A second, investment-related strategy focuses more directly on the children involved and attempts to augment skills (e.g., Head Start), improve health (e.g., WIC), or upgrade schools or other services. A third approach, argued cogently in Ellwood's (1988) book, is to make work "pay" through wage supplements and increases in the minimum wage. A general discussion of the various programs that might be directed at poor or otherwise at-risk children (e.g., Danziger and Weinberg, 1986; Ellwood, 1988) would take us far afield. We can, however, highlight policy implications of some of the less well-known aspects of the economic environment of childhood discussed thus far.

Persistent childhood poverty. Patterns of poverty throughout childhood show that single-year estimates of the poverty rate of children substantially understate the fraction of children who come into contact with poverty and overstate the extent of persistent childhood poverty. Without further research we cannot discount completely the possibly detrimental effect of temporary poverty. We can be more confident in pointing out the severe disadvantages associated with persistent child-hood poverty.

Persistent childhood poverty afflicts virtually no whites but nearly one-third of all Black children. It is found as often in rural as in urban areas and thus does not fit easily within the stereotype of an urban underclass. It is more heavily concentrated in single-parent families and yet is found often enough in intact families that raising the living standards or reducing the numbers of single-parent families alone will not solve the problem. Most of the persistently poor children live in situations in which parents have at best weak links to the labor market. Even so, there is enough work effort among the persistently poor to justify working toward further tax reform that would augment the incomes of low-income working families (Danziger, 1989a).

Income transfer programs such as AFDC and food stamps take on a new light in the context of the economic volatility we observe. Sharp declines in income are relatively widespread, but periods of need are often short. Correspondingly, longitudinal data show that periods of actual receipt of welfare program transfers are equally short. Only about one-sixth of all AFDC periods last more than eight years, and fewer than one-third of first-time recipients will have total welfare "careers" lasting that long (Ellwood, 1986).

Even Charles Murray, whose book *Losing Ground* led the conservative attack on Great Society welfare programs, now admits that current programs appear to function as benign income-loss insurance programs for many, and perhaps most, recipients (Murray, 1986).

Persistently poor children are more likely to live in the minority of long-term recipient households. Whether the programs themselves are responsible for inducing dependence in long-term recipients is an unresolved and obviously important question. At some point, however, concern over the possible dependence of the parents must be balanced against concern for the detrimental effects of persistent poverty on their children. Recent pushes for welfare reforms are encouraging but should not be viewed as a necessary precondition to channeling more resources to the children in greatest need of them.

Income volatility.   In addition to examining the level of resources available during childhood, especially the levels associated with persistent poverty, we have also focused on the incidence of large income losses at other points of the income distribution. The majority of such losses left the families involved with modest incomes, and most of them happened to families who neither predicted them in advance nor had savings to help cushion their effects. As with persistent poverty, Black children shouldered the brunt of these income losses.

A different set of policy issues arises if the goal is to minimize the incidence and effects of preventable losses that reduce income to points above the poverty line. Here the focus is on policies tied to events producing the losses, as with unemployment compensation tied to job loss and child support tied to divorce. Political strategies differ from those directed exclusively at poor children because events producing income losses occur in working- and middle-class families as well as poor families and thus have a larger potential constituency.

One reading of social policy over the last half-century concludes that the Great Depression convinced the voting majority that private insurance did not offer sufficient protection against dramatic drops in their economic well-being (Burkhauser and Duncan, 1988a). The pillars of social insurance established then—Social Security and unemployment insurance—have since been supplemented with disability and health insurance.

Taken together, they produced a set of insurance programs that provide some degree of protection against the potentially catastrophic events of disability, unemployment, retirement, and illness in old age. While one can point to gaps in coverage or problems in implementation, by and large these programs have offered substantial protection to a worker, his or her nonworking spouse, and their children. In an America where births were almost always within marriage and divorce was rare, this type of insurance effectively equated protection accorded to workers and their children against dramatic drops in living standards.

Today, however, the prevalence of divorce, separation and out-of-wedlock births has increased dramatically the proportion of children living in female-headed families. The social insurance programs, principally Aid to Families with Dependent Children, have been woefully inadequate to deal with the economic problems of single-parent families. Private "insurance" in the form of court-ordered child support and alimony payments is even less adequate. Tougher enforcement of court orders, coupled with a government-provided minimum child-support payment (Garfinkel and McLanahan, 1986), would go a long way toward treating certain types of marital dissolutions as a "socially insurable" risk where insurance could be financed in a manner similar to socially insurable labor-market risks.

NOTES

Portions of this chapter are drawn from "The Economic Environment of Childhood," in *Children in Poverty*, ed. Aletha Huston (New York: Cambridge University Press, 1992), and are here republished with permission. Preparation of the chapter was supported by the Ford Foundation. Sheldon Danziger and John Palmer made helpful suggestions on earlier drafts.

1. The best source of statistical information about poverty in the United States is the so-called "P-60 Series" of *Current Population Reports,* issued by the Bureau of the Census. These figures come from report no. 166 in the series.
2. Poverty is defined in the United States by a comparison of total family income and a poverty threshold based primarily on family size. The poverty threshold for a family of four in 1988 was about $12,000. International figures in Table 1 for other countries are based on an identical set of thresholds, with incomes converted to dollars with a multi-year average exchange rate (see Smeeding, 1988). Poverty rates for children in 1969 and 1979 differ slightly between Tables 1 and 2 because they are based on different Census Bureau surveys.
3. The poverty rates of families with children shown in Table 3 differ from those for children themselves shown in Table 2. Table 3 counts each family once, while Table 2 effectively counts each family by the number of children it contains. Since poverty rates for families with large numbers of children are higher than rates for families with fewer children, poverty rates for children exceed those of families with children.
4. As shown by Bane and Jargowsky (1987), the increased geographic concentration of poverty does not characterize all large cities and instead occurs mostly among the very largest cities in the Northeast and Midwest, especially New York, Philadelphia, Detroit, and Chicago.
5. Elder, 1974; Elder, 1979; Elder and Liker, 1982; Elder, Liker, and Cross, 1984; Elder, Liker, and Jaworski, 1984; Liker and Elder, 1983. Longitudinal evidence linking adverse income change to mental health is also presented in Perlin et al., 1981.

BIBLIOGRAPHY

Bane, M. J. (1986). "Household Composition and Poverty." In *Fighting Poverty: What Works and What Doesn't,* ed. S. Danziger and D. Weinberg. Cambridge: Harvard University Press.

Bane, M. J., and Ellwood, D. T. (1986). "Slipping Into and Out of Poverty: The Dynamics of Spells." *Journal of Human Resources* 21 (Winter): 1–23.

Bane, M. J., and Jargowsky, P. (1987). "Urban Poverty and the Underclass: Basic Questions." APPAM conference paper (October).

Burkhauser, R. V., and Duncan, G. J. (1988a). "Life Events, Public Policy and Economic Vulnerability of Children and the Elderly." In *The Vulnerable Americans: The Future of Support for Children and the Elderly,* ed. J. Palmer and T. Smeeding. Washington, DC: Urban Institute Press.

Burkhauser, R. V., and Duncan, G. J. (1988b). "Economic Risks of Gender Roles." *Social Science Quarterly* 70, no. 1 (August): 3–23.

Committee on Ways and Means. (1990). Background material and data on progress within the jurisdiction of the Committee on Ways and Means. Washington, DC: U.S. Government Printing Office.

Congressional Budget Office. (1988). *Trends in Family Income: 1970–1986.* Washington, DC: CBO.

Corcoran, M., and Hill, M. S. (1979). "The Incidence and Consequences of Short-and Longer-Run Unemployment." In *Five Thousand American Families,* Vol. 7, ed. G. J. Duncan and J. N. Morgan. Ann Arbor: Institute for Social Research.

Corcoran, M., et al. (1987). "Intergenerational Transmission of Education, Income and Earnings: Final Report to the Ford Foundation." Ann Arbor: University of Michigan, Institute for Public Policy Studies.

Danziger, S. (1989a). "Fighting Poverty and Reducing Welfare Dependency." In *Welfare Policy for the 1990s,* ed. P. Cunningham and D. Ellwood. Cambridge: Harvard University Press.

Danziger, S. (1989b). "Antipoverty Policies and Child Poverty." Discussion paper, University of Wisconsin, Institute for Research on Poverty.

Danziger S., and Gottschalk, P. (1985). "How Have Families with Children Been Faring?" Discussion paper, University of Wisconsin, Institute for Research on Poverty.

Danziger, S., and Weinberg, D. (1986). *Fighting Poverty: What Works and What Doesn't.* Cambridge: Harvard University Press.

Duncan, G. J. (1988). "Volatility of the Family Over the Life Course." In *Life-Span Development and Behavior,* Vol. 9, ed. P. Baltes, D. Featherman, and R. M. Lerner. Hillsdale, NJ: Lawrence Erlbaum Associates.

Duncan, G. J., and Rodgers, W. (1988). "Longitudinal Aspects of Childhood Poverty." *Journal of Marriage and the Family* 50 (November): 1007–21).

Elder, G. H. (1974). *Children of the Great Depression.* Chicago: University of Chicago Press.

Elder, G. H. (1979). "Historical Change in Life Patterns and Personality." In *Life-Span Development and Behavior*, Vol. 2, ed. P. B. Baltes and O. G. Brim, Jr. New York: Academic Press.

Elder, G. H., and Liker, J. K. (1982). "Hard Times in Women's Lives: Historical Influences Across Fifty Years." *American Journal of Sociology* 88: 241–69.

Elder, G. H., Liker, J. K., and Cross, C. E. (1984). "Parent-Child Behavior in the Great Depression: Life Course and Intergenerational Influences." In *Life-Span Development and Behavior*, Vol. 6, ed. P. B. Baltes and O. G. Brim, Jr. New York: Academic Press.

Elder, G. H., Liker, J. K., and Jaworski, B. J. (1984). "Hardship in Lives: Depression Influences in the 1930s to Old Age in Postwar America." In *Life-Span Development Psychology: Historical and Generational Effects,* ed. K. A. McCluskey and H. W. Reese. New York: Academic Press.

Ellwood, D. T. (1986). *Targeting Would-Be Long-Term Recipients of AFDC: Who Should Be Served?* Princeton, NJ: Mathematica Policy Research.

Ellwood, D. T. (1988). *Poor Support: Poverty in the American Family.* New York: Basic Books.

Garfinkel, I., and McLanahan, S. (1986). *Single Mothers and Their Children: A New American Dilemma.* Washington, DC: Urban Institute Press.

Gottschalk, P., and Danziger, S. (1985). "A Framework for Evaluating the Effects of Economic Growth and Transfers on Poverty." *American Economic Review* 75, no. 1 (March): 153–61.

Hill, M. S., (1983). "Trends in the Economic Situation of U.S. Families and Children: 1970–1980." In *American Families and the Economy: The High Cost of Living*, ed. R. Nelson and F. Skidmore. Washington, DC: National Academy Press.

Hill, M. S. and Duncan, G. J. (1987). "Parental Family Income and the Socioeconomic Attainment of Children." *Social Science Research* 16, 39–73.

Hill, M. S., et al. (1985). *Motivation and Economic Mobility.* Ann Arbor: Institute for Social Research, Research Report Series.

Hoffman, S. D., and Duncan, G. J. (1988). "What Are the Economic Consequences of Divorce?" *Demography* 25, no. 4 (November): 641–45.

Levy, F. (1988). *Dollars and Dreams: The Changing American Income Distribution.* New York: Russell Sage Foundation.

Liker, J. K., and Elder, G. H. (1983). "Economic Hardship and Marital Relations in the 1930's." *American Sociological Review* 48: 343–59.

McLanahan, S. (1985). "Family Structure and the Reproduction of Poverty." *American Journal of Sociology* 90: 873–901.

Murray, C. (1986). "According to Age: Longitudinal Profiles of AFDC Recipients and the Poor by Age Group." Paper prepared for the Working Seminar on the Family and American Welfare Policy, Washington, DC (September).

Murray, C. A. (1984). *Losing Ground: American Social Policy, 1950–1980.* New York: Basic Books.

Perlin, L. I., Liberman, M. A., Menaghan, E. F., and Mullan, J. (1981). "The Stress Process." *Journal of Health and Social Behavior* 22: 337–56.

Phillips, Kevin (1990). *The Politics of Rich and Poor: Wealth and the American Electorate in the Reagan Aftermath.* New York: Random House.

Salkind, N. J., and Haskins, R. (1982). "Negative Income Tax: The Impact on Low-Income Families." *Journal of Family Issues* 34, no. 2 (June): 165–80.

Sewell, W. H., and Hauser, R. M. (1975). *Education, Occupation, and Earnings: Achievement in the Early Career.* New York: Academic Press.

Shaw, L. B. (1982). "High School Completion for Young Women." *Journal of Family Issues* 3, no. 2 (June).

Smeeding, T. M. (1988). "The Children of Poverty: The Evidence on Poverty and Comparative Income Support Policies in Eight Countries." Testimony before the Select Committee on Children, Youth and Families, U.S. House of Representatives (Feb. 25).

Wilson, W. J. (1987). *The Truly Disadvantaged.* Chicago: University of Chicago Press.

2

Welfare Dependence within and across Generations

Greg J. Duncan, Martha S. Hill, and Saul D. Hoffman

Corridor Courtyard, lithograph

Few social issues generate more concern and debate than the question of how our country should assist its poorest citizens. During the past several decades, growth in total spending on assistance programs, in the number of families headed by women, and in the perceived size of the urban underclass has combined with stubbornly persistent poverty rates, especially among children, to fuel speculation that the assistance programs themselves are responsible for such trends. In his 1986 State of the Union address, President Reagan charged that poverty programs

29

have created "a spider web of dependency," fostering a welfare culture in which the "breakdown of the family . . . has reached crisis proportions."[1]

Many programs that provide benefits to families with low incomes and assets fall under the "welfare" rubric. Our focus is on the best known and most criticized program: Aid to Families with Dependent Children (AFDC). AFDC offers assistance to families with children, primarily those families headed by a single parent (usually the mother). States have considerable freedom in setting benefit levels and other program features; this results in maximum monthly grants varying (in January 1987 for a family of four) from $144 in Mississippi to $706 in New York. Some states extend AFDC benefits to two-parent families in which the principal wage earner is unemployed, but these instances amount to a small percentage of the total caseload. In 1986, expenditures on AFDC totaled nearly $18 billion, and 3.8 million families received payments.

The argument that welfare fosters dependence arises from two concerns: that the welfare system alters the choices people face and encourages them to behave in ways that increase their likelihood of receipt; and that the system fosters a welfare culture by creating dependence and discouraging self-sufficiency in both recipient parents and their children. Either or both may result in welfare having adverse effects on childbearing, marital and family ties, and work effort. Counterbalancing this negative view is the idea that welfare is an investment in children that provides additional resources to parents to improve the health and enhance the education of their children.

In this article, we examine the issues involved in the welfare debate, using a number of recent studies on AFDC receipt within and across generations. A decade ago there were virtually no sources of nationally representative information on long-run welfare experiences, but now there are several. The primary sources include longitudinal survey studies that have followed nationally representative samples of both recipients and nonrecipients and their children for fifteen or more years. Others draw their data from welfare caseload records.

In summarizing the current state of knowledge about each of these issues, we first discuss patterns of welfare receipt, turn next to findings on the effects of welfare on behavior, attitudes, and values, and conclude with evidence about the effects of welfare on the attainments of children.

PATTERNS OF WELFARE RECEIPT

Some case studies of families receiving welfare provide vivid and memorable accounts of long-term dependence. But such case studies are selected to illustrate instances of long-term dependence. Whether they represent the experiences of typical recipients is an issue that needs to be addressed first. If most welfare receipt is long term, then the issue of welfare dependence arises, and it is important to determine whether the welfare system itself plays any role in creating that dependence. But if most people ever receiving welfare do so for only a short time, then the welfare system might better be regarded as providing most recipients with short-term insurance against income losses, such as those resulting from unemployment or divorce.

Estimates of total time on welfare can be calculated either for all individuals who ever received welfare or for individuals on welfare at a given point in time.[2] Table 1 shows the distribution of time on AFDC for individuals who first entered the welfare rolls between the mid-1960s and the late 1970s, a sample of "ever on" recipients. The estimates of total time on welfare indicate that about 30 percent of recipients received welfare for one or two years, and a similar proportion had eight or more total years of receipt. The median length of receipt was less than four years. Clearly, long-term welfare usage characterizes only a minority of recipients.

Table 1 also shows results for a point-in-time sample that presents a very different picture of the typical pattern of receipt. Very short periods of receipt characterize 7 percent of point-in-time recipients, whereas nearly two-thirds are in the midst of long-term welfare usage, totaling eight or more years. Thus, longer-term recipients account for the bulk of individuals receiving welfare at a particular time.

While the large difference between the two methods of calculation may seem paradoxical, it is easily explained and, indeed, is characteristic of other phenomena such as poverty, unemployment, or hospitalization. The difference occurs because the probability of being in a given status (for example, on welfare) at any point in time is necessarily higher for individuals who occupy that status longer. Thus, point-in-time samples of welfare recipients yield biased information on the typical experiences of welfare recipients.

Welfare experiences differ markedly among different AFDC recipients. For example, among the recipients who, when first on AFDC,

Table 1
Distribution of length of total time of AFDC

Years	Persons ever on AFDC (%)	Persons on AFDC at a given time (%)
1–2	30	7
3–7	40	28
≥8	30	65
Total	100	100

Note: The data were compiled from D. Ellwood, "Targeting the Would-Be Long-Term Recipient of AFDC: Who Should be Served?" (Princeton, NJ: Mathematica Policy Research, 1986).

were twenty-five years of age or older and had previous work experience and a high-school degree, fewer than one in seven eventually received AFDC for as many as nine years.[3] On the other hand, total duration of welfare receipt is quite long for younger, never-married recipients. More than 40 percent of the never-married women with young children who first received AFDC before age twenty-five received it for nine or more years. Whether welfare plays a much less benign role in affecting the behavior and attitudes of this latter set of women is a crucial, and as yet largely unanswered, question.

The social circumstances and economic positions of women before and after their periods of welfare receipt are quite diverse.[4] Divorce is the most common event associated with the beginning of a period of receipt, typically drawing from women whose pre-divorce family incomes were in the bottom half of the income distribution. A substantial minority of women who stop receiving welfare have incomes below the poverty level at least once in the years following receipt; such poverty experiences are especially prevalent among women who stopped receiving welfare because their families no longer contained minor children.

DOES WELFARE AFFECT BEHAVIOR?

The fact that many brushes with the welfare system are short-lived indicates that welfare receipt does not lead inevitably to long-term dependence. However, to assess the welfare system properly, one needs to go beyond descriptive evidence on patterns of usage and consider whether the welfare system itself adversely affects the work, family structure, and other behavior of recipients and their children, particularly the minority who are long-term recipients. Consider, for example, the types of events that initiate periods of welfare usage. Most involve changes in family structure, with divorces and separations accounting for nearly half and out-of-wedlock births accounting for one-third of all beginnings of periods of welfare receipt.[5] If the availability or generosity of welfare causes these demographic events to occur more frequently, then concerns about adverse effects of welfare are bolstered, especially if the impact is substantial.

The evidence compiled to date on these behavioral effects suggests that welfare has little systematic impact on family structure, although it does indeed seem to reduce work effort.

Welfare and work hours.   The economic theory of labor supply suggests that welfare programs such as AFDC should reduce the work effort of potential recipients. Such programs simultaneously increase unearned income and, by reducing benefits for added dollars of earned income, lower the recipient's net hourly wage rate.

Evidence consistently indicates that income transfer programs do indeed reduce labor supply, but estimates vary widely as to the size of the effect. According to one recent review of the evidence, AFDC reduces the average annual work effort among female heads of households by 180 hours.[6]

Welfare and family structure.   Because AFDC benefits are generally available only to women heading households with dependent children, they are alleged to encourage marital instability and illegitimate births, while discouraging marriage and remarriage.

The many studies of the possible effects of AFDC on family structure are not entirely conclusive. One of the most recent and comprehensive studies examines a lengthy list of family structure variables with several sources of data.[7] Amounts of AFDC payments are found to have no measurable impact on births to unmarried women and only a modest effect on rates of divorce, separation, or female head-of-household status. The biggest impact is on a relatively unnoticed family decision—the living arrangements of single mothers. In states with high AFDC benefit amounts, the relative chances that young, unmarried mothers would be living independently rather than in the home of a parent were greater. Thus, AFDC appears to have its greatest impact on less (socially) significant decisions such as living arrangements, with no measurable impact on the most significant and far-reaching family decision —the birth of a child.

DOES WELFARE AFFECT VALUES AND ATTITUDES?

Apart from possible effects on the relative attractiveness of work and family choices, welfare programs are also thought to induce dependence by changing the attitudes and values of recipients and their children. In this respect, arguments about a welfare culture share a great deal with theories of poverty cultures that gained prominence in the 1960s. Proponents of such cultural views held that the poor exhibit a number of psychological traits—weak sense of control over events, orientation toward the present rather than the future—and behaviors that leave them unable to take advantage of opportunities and keep them mired in poverty. Furthermore, these undesirable traits and behaviors are allegedly passed on from parent to child, perpetuating dependence across generations.[8] These views have resurfaced in recent analyses of welfare recipients. Although rich with predictions, theories of welfare dependence that posit an important role for personality factors within and across generations are only beginning to be tested in a systematic way.

Attitudes and values of adults. In assessing the effects of welfare on adults, it is not enough to observe that the attitudes and values of long-term welfare recipients are somehow "worse" than those of other people. Although such attitudinal differences may indeed have been caused by welfare receipt, they may instead have preceded and caused the welfare receipt. Or it may be that both the psychological traits and the welfare receipt are caused by some other factor, such as disability or residence in a high-unemployment area.

A truly consistent linkage between welfare receipt and psychological characteristics would require meeting three criteria: that recipients have measurably "worse" values and attitudes, that attitudes and values are affected adversely by welfare receipt, and that the initially worse values and attitudes increase the likelihood of future dependence.

A number of researchers have attempted to use nationally representative survey data to identify attitudes that are changed by welfare receipt and that affect the likelihood of further receipt. Social-psycholog-
ical measures available in these data sets include personal efficacy (the
extent to which a person feels in control of events), orientation toward
the future, and more basic achievement motives such as challenge,
power, and affiliation.

The research has found evidence of a bivariate association between
welfare and some negative attitudes of recipients. Women, especially
white women, who receive income from welfare feel less in control of
their lives and are less oriented toward the future than those not receiving welfare.[9] But evidence from several studies, although not conclusive, shows no causal role for welfare in producing these attitudes; also,
these attitudes were not shown to affect subsequent economic success.
There is no consistent evidence that experience with AFDC causes significant change in either sense of control or future orientation.[10] In addition, women with lower initial scores on the psychological measures
usually have subsequent welfare and labor-market experiences indistin-
guishable from those of other women.

Intergenerational transmission of welfare dependence. There is great
interest in possible intergenerational effects of welfare receipt, especially
the extent to which children growing up in welfare-recipient households are themselves more likely to receive welfare when they become
adults. Theories of poverty have often included an intergenerational
component, and this has fostered beliefs of a similar process in welfare
use. In his writings on the culture of poverty in the late 1960s, Lewis
observed that slum children by age six or seven "have usually absorbed
the basic values and attitudes of their subculture and are not psychologically geared to take full advantage of the changing conditions or increased opportunities that may occur in their lifetime."[11]

In the debate over the culture-of-poverty theories, some scholars
have aligned themselves with either the cultural perspective or the
structural perspective.[12] The most extreme cultural view holds that
counterproductive values and attitudes of parents are passed to their
children through early socialization and that these persist into adulthood. A somewhat less deterministic cultural view not only extends the
socialization role to the wider environment, such as the neighborhood

in which the children are raised, and covers the entire childhood period, but also argues that these childhood experiences guide development into adulthood. In either case, to the extent that welfare processes are similar to poverty processes, the cultural perspective suggests an important role for a welfare culture in the values and attitudes of children raised in dependent homes.

The structural view of the link of welfare dependence across generations holds that the values and attitudes of children raised in dependent homes or in neighborhoods with high concentrations of welfare families are not significantly different from those of other children. Instead, according to this view, these children develop values and attitudes that are different from those of others when they later encounter the same kinds of structural impediments to jobs and marriages (such as discrimination or poor employment opportunities) that had blocked their parents.

The data needed to sort out cultural and structural explanations consist of measurements of attitudes and values, of welfare use, and of environmental conditions of both parents and children taken at several points in the children's lives, from birth to adulthood. Such data do not currently exist for the United States. Indeed, only in the last several years have there been reliable measurements from a national sample of the simple associations between the welfare dependence of parents and their grown children. But even descriptive intergenerational information can help by providing a more accurate perspective for some of the graphic case studies of intergenerational dependence that periodically appear in the media.

Table 2 presents bivariate evidence on the intergenerational transmission of AFDC status; information from a nineteen-year longitudinal study of the economic fortunes of a large and representative sample of American families was used in the calculations. The subsample used for the figures presented in Table 2 consists of 1,085 daughters whose parents' economic status was observed while the daughters were between the ages of thirteen and fifteen; the economic status of the daughters was observed later, when they were between twenty-one and twenty-three years of age. The early teenage years are thought to be crucial for the socialization of children to adult roles and the formation of expectations that will guide future behavior, whereas the period between ages twenty-one and twenty-three should be indicative of the paths that the young women are following in early adulthood. For each of those two three-year periods, AFDC dependence was defined according to whether AFDC income was reported in none of the years (no dependence), in one or two years (moderate), or in all three years (high). These categories are less precise than the terms may imply because of the sporadic nature of many families' welfare use.

Table 2

Intergenerational patterns of AFDC receipt

Dependence of parents	Dependence of daughters (%)				Unweighted number of cases
	None	Moderate	High	Total	
None	91	6	3	100	811
Moderate	62	22	16	100	127
High	64	16	20	100	147

Note: Calculated by the authors from data on 736 welfare spells observed in the Panel Study of Income Dynamics, *User Guide to the Panel Study of Income Dynamics* (Ann Arbor: University of Michigan, Inter-university Consortium for Political and Social Research, 1984).

Despite the impression given by case studies focusing on multi-generational welfare use, the majority of daughters who grew up in highly dependent homes did not share the fate of their parents. Only one out of five (20 percent) of the daughters from highly dependent parental families were themselves highly dependent on AFDC in their early twenties; more than three out of five (64 percent) of the daughters with dependent backgrounds received no AFDC during the three-year period.[13] The stereotype of heavy welfare dependence being routinely passed from mother to child is thus contradicted by these data. Indeed, the diversity of attainments of children from disadvantaged backgrounds emerging from these data shows up in other longitudinal data sources as well.[14]

But at the same time, the data in Table 2 also show a higher incidence of dependence on welfare among women with welfare backgrounds. The fraction of daughters from highly dependent homes who themselves became highly dependent (20 percent) is much greater than the fraction of daughters from nonrecipient families who became highly dependent (3 percent).[15] And while more than three out of five of the daughters who grew up in AFDC-dependent homes received no AFDC themselves, more than nine-tenths of those who grew up in non-recipient families received no AFDC in their early adult years.

An obvious problem in using these figures to draw inferences about intergenerational transmission of welfare dependence is that they fail to adjust for other aspects of parental background and environment that may also affect the likelihood of AFDC receipt. Children from AFDC-dependent homes generally have fewer parental resources available to them, live in worse neighborhoods, go to lower-quality schools, and so forth. Any of these factors could affect their chances of receiving AFDC independently of the effect of their parents' AFDC receipt.

Consider, for example, what happens when we apply to daughters from nonrecipient families the same types of demographic restrictions that apply to most daughters from recipient families. If we look at daughters from low-income, nonrecipient parental families (income less than twice the official federal poverty line), the percentage highly dependent on welfare as adults rises to 7 percent, more than double the level for all daughters from nonrecipient families. The percentage dependent as adults doubles yet again, to 14 percent, if the sample is restricted to daughters who grew up in low-income, mother-only, non-recipient families. Clearly, the welfare dependence of these daughters as adults is affected by factors other than the welfare dependence of their parents, but as yet, fairly elaborate studies, while controlling for other factors, have been unable to estimate conclusively the extent to which welfare dependence is transmitted between generations.[16]

DOES WELFARE HELP OR HURT CHILDREN?

The more general intergenerational question is how income from welfare programs and other sources affects a variety of outcomes for children, such as their schooling, work effort, and career attainments. Children growing up in families with higher incomes appear to complete more schooling and gain higher-paying jobs, even after taking into account differences in parental schooling and occupational attainment.[17] Does income from welfare have a similar positive effect?

A handful of recent studies of the links between parental welfare receipt and the success of children based on nationally representative data found various effects. Studies of the completed schooling of children and their adult hourly earnings found mixed evidence that welfare income is as beneficial as other sources of income.[18] An investigation of the effects of parental welfare on the work effort of sons found no consistent effects.[19] Not enough is known, but the recent availability of background information at both the family and neighborhood levels promises to add greatly to our understanding of how these factors interact to affect children's lives.

CAN DEPENDENCE BE REDUCED?

An important question is whether anything can be done to reduce dependence on welfare, particularly among long-term recipients, who account for the bulk of expenditures. Since only about one in five AFDC recipients receives child support from an absent father, an obvious strategy is more rigorous enforcement of existing child-support awards, although one estimate suggests this would reduce the number of AFDC recipients by only 5 percent. More ambitious schemes combining child-support enforcement with guaranteed minimum support payments would reduce caseloads much more.[20]

Other approaches include preventing the onset of AFDC receipt for likely long-term recipients and lessening the future dependence of current recipients. Programs aimed at preventing initial receipt (for example, by reducing the number of out-of-wedlock births or increasing the number of at-risk children completing high school) have not proved consistently successful.[21] However, there is mounting evidence that a variety of job-search and training programs for long-term recipients have results that are cost-effective, although substantively modest.

The brevity of most AFDC experiences makes the task of evaluating intervention programs especially difficult. If directed at first-time applicants, even ineffective programs might appear successful because the duration of welfare use for many persons is so short. Random assignment between treatment and control groups is crucial for a proper evaluation of intervention programs and has been incorporated into a number of job-search and training programs.[22] Taken together, these evaluations suggest that both job-search and training programs increase the employment and earnings of participating individuals relative to control-group individuals; that the increases in employment and earnings are, however, modest (the fraction of individuals with jobs increases by 3 to 9 percentage points, and individuals' annual earnings increase by $100 to $600, the equivalent of 8 percent to 36 percent gains); that programs directed at long-term recipient women are typically more successful than those programs directed at unemployed men or at women with recent work experience; and that programs administered in rural areas, particularly those areas with very high unemployment, are less successful than those administered in the typically urban economic environments. A major question concerns the relative benefits of lower-cost job-search programs versus more expensive training programs.

CONCLUSION

The current debate over welfare programs generates strikingly different opinions about relative costs and benefits of public assistance. To what extent does welfare reduce recipient motivation to work or to marry, encourage recipients to have children, impair their attitudes, or otherwise trap them in dependence? How important are the benefits that result from the resources welfare provides to low-income families?

Evidence on the nature of welfare experiences overall shows that a surprisingly large proportion of welfare experiences are short-lived, that the typical total length of welfare receipt is less than four years, and that most children growing up in heavily dependent homes do not become heavily dependent as adults. This evidence suggests that the welfare system does not foster reliance on welfare so much as it acts as insurance against temporary misfortune.

Although long-term recipients constitute a minority of all individuals who ever receive welfare, the fact that more than 2 million families are persistently dependent on welfare raises questions of whether welfare itself promotes divorce or out-of-wedlock births, discourages marriage, erodes work effort, or instills counterproductive attitudes and values that encourage reliance on welfare. Although welfare programs do indeed appear to reduce work effort to some extent, the sparse evidence fails to show any connection between welfare and attitudes. As yet unresolved questions include the extent to which welfare affects family decisions and whether dependence during childhood, within either families or neighborhoods, creates dependence in adulthood.

NOTES

"Welfare Dependence within and across Generations" first appeared in *Science* 239 (29 Jan. 1988): 467–71, © 1988 by the American Association for the Advancement of Science, and is here republished with permission.

This work was supported in part by a grant from the Ford Foundation. The collection of data in the Panel Study of Income Dynamics project has been supported by the National Science Foundation and the United States Department of Health and Human Services. We gratefully acknowledge comments on earlier drafts by M. Corcoran, J. Gueron, P. Gurin, H. Hartmann, J. House, C. Jencks, S. Kennedy, J. Liker, J. Morgan, M. Ponza, R. Sarri, H. Schuman, G. Solon, and D. Weinberg and the research assistance of D. Laren and G. Burpee.

1. Transcript of Reagan's speech to Congress on the State of the Union, *New York Times*, 5 February 1986, p. 10. That such concerns transcend ideology and time is reflected in Reagan's quotation from President Franklin D. Roosevelt's 1935 State of the Union address: "Welfare is a narcotic, a subtle destroyer of the human spirit."

2. Estimates of total time on welfare are taken from D. Ellwood, "Targeting the Would-Be Long-Term Recipient of AFDC: Who Should Be Served?" (Princeton, NJ: Mathematica Policy Research, 1986). They are simulations of the likely total number of years of receipt of welfare during the twenty-five-year period following initial receipt. M. J. Bane and D. Ellwood ("The Dynamics of Dependence: The Routes to Self-Sufficiency" [Cambridge, MA: Urban Systems Research and Engineering, 1983]) were the first researchers to cast welfare experiences in terms of completed periods of receipt and to develop many of the insights included in this discussion.

3. The estimates in this paragraph are from Ellwood, "Targeting" (Table IV.2).

4. Economic status after welfare receipt is analyzed by Bane and Ellwood, "Dynamics," and C. Murray, "According to Age: Longitudinal Profiles of AFDC Recipients and the Poor by Age Group" (Paper prepared for the Working Seminar on the Family and American Welfare Policy, Washington, DC, September 1986). The links between economic status, welfare receipt, and divorce are analyzed by G. Duncan and S. Hoffman in *Horizontal Equity, Uncertainty and Well-Being,* ed. M. David and T. Smeeding (Chicago: University of Chicago Press, 1985), 427–67.

5. Studies of distinct periods of welfare receipt include Bane and Ellwood,

"Dynamics"; Ellwood, "Targeting"; and J. O'Neill, D. Wolf, L. Bassi, and M. Hannan, "An Analysis of Time on Welfare" (Washington, DC: Urban Institute, June 1984). The figures for family-related events come from Bane and Ellwood.

6. The AFDC estimate is made by S. Danziger, R. Haveman, and R. Plotnick, "How Income Transfer Programs Affect Work, Savings and the Income Distribution: A Critical Review," *Journal of Economic Literature* 19 (1981): 975. A more complete review of the labor-supply literature is given in M. Killingsworth, *Labor Supply* (New York: Cambridge University Press, 1983).

7. D. Ellwood and M. J. Bane, in *Research in Labor Economics*, vol. 7, ed. R. Ehrenberg (Greenwich, CT: JAI Press, 1985), 137–207.

8. The debate on the cultural view is reviewed in J. T. Patterson, *America's Struggle Against Poverty, 1900–1980* (Cambridge: Harvard University Press, 1981).

9. See, for example, M. S. Hill et al., *Motivation and Economic Mobility* (Ann Arbor: Survey Research Center, ISR Research Report Series, 1985), Table 5.2.

10. These conclusions were reached in the two most comprehensive studies that use representative survey data: Hill et al., *Motivation,* and O'Neill et al., "Analysis." Although the two studies agree in finding little consistent effect of efficacy and future orientation on subsequent success, the Hill et al. study found some evidence that the challenge motive (not measured in the O'Neill et al. study) did affect the subsequent success of Black women and their children. The O'Neill et al. study found no evidence that experience with AFDC reduced either sense of control or future orientation; the Hill et al. study found marginally significant effects of AFDC receipt on changes in sense of control for white women.

11. O. Lewis, *La Vida, A Puerto Rican Family in the Culture of Poverty: San Juan and New York* (London: Panther Books, 1968), 5–6.

12. The cultural and structural models of poverty are contrasted by J. House in *Social Psychology: Sociological Perspective*, ed. M. Rosenberg and R. Turner (New York: Basic Books, 1981), 525–61.

13. Patterns in Table 2 are consistent with intergenerational information based on longer intervals and different definitions of dependence used by Hill et al., *Motivation.*

14. One notable example is a seventeen-year follow-up study of teenage mothers who grew up in a poor neighborhood in Baltimore, described by F. Furstenberg, Jr., J. Brooks-Gunn, and J. P. Morgan, *Adolescent Mothers in Later Life* (New York: Cambridge University Press, 1987).

15. This and all other differences cited in the text about the figures in Table 2 are statistically significant at the 5 percent probability level.

16. M. S. Hill et al., *Motivation*, and M. S. Hill and M. Ponza, "Does Welfare Dependence Beget Dependency?" (Ann Arbor: University of Michigan, Institute for Social Research, 1984), find insignificant effects, while S. McLanahan (*Demography*, in press) finds more significant effects.

17. This result has been obtained with a number of different intergenerational data sets that contain reliable measures of parental income; see, for example, W. Sewell and R. Hauser, *Education, Occupation and Earnings: Achievement in the Early Career* (New York: Academic Press, 1975), and M. S. Hill and G. J. Duncan, "Income and the Socioeconomic Attainment of Children," *Social Science Research* 16 (1987): 39.

18. M. S. Hill and G. J. Duncan, "Income and the Socioeconomic Attainment of Children," examine the effects of welfare on both completed schooling and wages, and S. McLanahan, "Family Structure and the Reproduction of Poverty," *The American Journal of Sociology* 90 (1985): 873, focuses on schooling activities.

19. See Hill and Ponza, "Welfare Dependence."

20. See I. Garfinkel and S. McLanahan, *Single Mothers and Their Children* (Washington, DC: Urban Institute, 1986), and P. Robins, "Child Support, Welfare Dependency, and Poverty," *American Economic Review* 76 (1986): 768, for a discussion of the child-support system and proposals for reform.

21. National Research Council Panel on Adolescent Pregnancy and Childbearing, *Risking the Future: Adolescent Sexuality, Pregnancy, and Childbearing* (Washington, DC: National Academy Press, 1987).

22. Findings from a variety of such programs are reviewed in J. Guerson, *Work Initiatives for Welfare Recipients: Lessons from a Multi-State Experiment* (New York: Manpower Demonstration Research Corporation, 1986), and J. Grossman et al., "Reanalysis of the Effects of Selected Employment and Training Programs for Welfare Recipients" (Princeton, NJ: Mathematica Policy Research, 1985).

II

Theological Analyses of Poverty

Joanne's Old Boy Friend, lithograph

3

Poverty, Womanist Theology, and the Ministry of the Church

Jacquelyn Grant

At the end of Alice Walker's book *The Color Purple,* her character Celie has been broadened by her evolving perception of God. Having been liberated from the Western, static understanding of a male God, she goes back to affirming her African heritage of experiencing God through the symbols that God created. She concludes after a long journey: "Dear God. Dear stars, dear trees, dear sky, dear people. Dear Everything, Dear God."[1]

After a life of powerlessness, Celie is empowered to affirm life even in herself. When the children begin to look at her and the host of characters as "old and don't know much what going on," even Celie can say, "But I don't think us feel old at all. And us so happy. Matter of fact, I think this the youngest us ever felt."[2]

No one else can define these heavenly realities that Celie now calls her own. Black women must define these for themselves—but the realities are external and therefore subject to public participation and scrutiny. Since Black women's experiences of the heavenly realities are unique, they must give their own testimony. No one can do it for them; no one *will* do it for them. For the most part, the voices of Black women have been silenced and rendered socially, politically, and economically powerless.

I see wrapped up in one of Maya Angelou's poems, "Woman Work," both the powerlessness and the power of Black women.[3] The powerlessness is reflected in the fact that Black women have no control

47

over their world of work with children, employers, house care, and food preparation. The external power that controls Black women is a complex sociopolitical and economic system that defines for women in general and Black women in particular their work world inside and outside the home. Obviously, then, the historic power of women must be substantially located in realities that are in some significant way independent of the system. Therein lies the source of empowerment.

What is the source of powerlessness? What is the source of power? I wish to explore these questions by addressing the racialization of poverty, the feminization of poverty, and the theological mandate for the church.

First, I explore the relationship between racism and poverty by asking the question, What role does racism play in the institutionalization and perpetuation of poverty?

Second, I address the same question in relationship to sexism. I explore the ways in which some have argued that there is a particular relationship between women and poverty and specifically that poverty has taken on a feminine face.

Third, I reflect upon the implications of the racialization and feminization of poverty for doing theology today. This discussion provides several insights into womanist theology, the question of poverty, and the ministry of the church.

THE RACIALIZATION OF POVERTY

Poverty is not only a national phenomenon that has reached crisis proportions, it is also a global one. North Americans have become accustomed to seeing electronic images of international poverty—swollen bellies of malnourished children, shanty-style living conditions, high infant mortality rates resulting from poor health care during pregnancy and after birth, chronic illness and premature death resulting from inaccessibility of health care. The inclination of many "charity"-oriented North Americans is to make contributions to help the needy in the Third World or so-called developing countries. However, the gaunt international faces of poverty do not lessen the impact and pain of those faces in our own nation. The scourge of domestic poverty is much closer to us than these questionable, guilt-laden appeals for legitimate global aid.

Because poverty is a national and an international issue, in what sense is it meaningful to speak of the racialization of poverty in the North American context? Is not poverty the same everywhere? Is it not a category unto itself, without racial- or gender-specific realities? Scholars have answered these questions in the negative.

Serious examinations reveal that racism impacts poverty in significant and extremely negative ways. Two generalizations can be made: (1) poverty in the United States is overwhelmingly Black, and (2) the elimination of poverty is impossible without a serious struggle against the racist oppression that generates much of it.

Consider the situation of African-Americans in the United States. It has been well documented that racism manifests itself in all aspects of American life. Politically, racism disenfranchises; socially, it ostracizes; culturally, it degrades and robs the people of those characteristics that make them a people; religiously, it brainwashes and indoctrinates so that the oppressed peoples believe not only that it is impossible for God to look like them or for them to image God, but also that God ordains racist oppression. It stands to reason that these manifestations would have crippling economic effects.

Michael Harrington in *The Other American* describes racism and poverty in the following way:

The American economy, the American society, the American unconscious are all racist. If all the laws were framed to provide equal opportunity, a majority of the Negroes would not be able to take full advantage of the change. There would still be a vast, silent, and automatic system directed against men and women of color.[4]

Since the initial publication of Harrington's book in 1962, this has certainly been born out. Legislation regarding education, civil rights, and affirmative action has not enabled Black people "to take full advantage of the change[s made]." Harrington continues:

To belong to a racial minority is to be poor. . . . The fear, the lack of self-confidence, the haunting . . . {characterize the life of the poor}. But they, in turn, are the expressions of the most institutionalized poverty in the United States, the most vicious of the vicious circle. In a sense, the Negro is classically the "other"

American, degraded and frustrated at every turn and not just
because of laws.[5]

Harrington emphasizes how racism is so ingrained in American society that many people inappropriately compare the plight of Blacks
with white groups such as the Irish, the Italians, and the Jews. These
wishful critics postulate that just as these groups have "made it" in
American society, given time and hard work, Blacks should also. Harrington challenges this naïveté:

This notion misses two decisive facts: that the Negro is colored,
and no other group in the United States has ever faced such a
problem, and that the Negro of today is an internal migrant
who will face racism wherever he goes, who cannot leave his op-
pression behind as if it were a czar or a potato famine. To be
equal, the Negro requires something much more profound than a
way "into" the society; he {or she} needs a transformation of
some of the basic institutions of the society.[6]

In other words, racism is so profound and pervasive in North
America that it results in African-Americans being placed in a unique
position unlike that of any other European immigrant to the continent.
Whereas the possibility for escape exists for European immigrants,
African-Americans, by virtue of color, are locked into their state of oppression. Nothing short of total transformation is required to effectively
eliminate the structural and interstructural oppression that victimizes
Black people. The covert and overt racism, the direct and indirect racism, and the many expressions of racism in between will remain unless
they are adequately and consistently challenged at the structural level.

What are the measures of poverty that illustrate the integral relationship between racism and poverty? According to scholars such as
Theodore Cross (in *The Black Power Imperative*), Blacks are three times as
likely to live in poverty than whites. Even during periods when poverty
rates are slightly lower, the percentage of Black families in poverty
compared to white families is still about three to one. According to the
U.S. Department of Commerce, Bureau of the Census, in 1954 Black
families represented a little more than 45 percent of the families in pov-

erty, whereas white families represented less than 15 percent of families in poverty. In 1984, even though Black families made up only about 11 percent of all families, more than 28 percent of them were classified as living in poverty.[7]

Some critics have pointed to the high percentage of female-headed households as the most significant factor in the Black poverty rate. In response to this charge, Cross provides data that demonstrate that Black "intact" families, or families headed by men, are still overwhelmingly poor in relation to white intact families. In 1984, more than 43 percent of all Black families were headed by females, as compared with 13 percent of white families. The poverty rate for Black families headed by women was 51.7 percent, compared with only 27.1 percent for white single-female-parent families. Black single-female-adult families accounted for 73 percent of all Black families in poverty, about 44 percent of all female-headed families in poverty, and more than 21 percent of all families in poverty—white and Black, male- and female-headed.[8] In the Black context, the absence of a male does seriously impact the status of the family. Yet it is not the whole story. Another look at the statistics reveals that in 1984, 6.4 percent of white "intact" families lived in poverty, while the rate of poverty for Black intact families was 14.7 percent. Black families in poverty still outnumber white families in poverty two to one.

In attempting to explicate Black poverty some have used the variables of age, family size, and education to justify the disproportional representation between the races. Cross therefore compares the data in each category for whites and Blacks. When these variables are held constant for both races, he finds that Black families still experience a higher rate of poverty: at least two to one. Black family heads in the twenty-five and under age group are 2.6 times more likely to live in poverty than are whites. In the fifty-five to fifty-nine age group, Black heads of families are 4.1 times more likely to live in poverty than are whites.

When families are studied according to size, Cross finds comparable results. Regardless of the size of Black families, poverty runs from 2.1 to 3.5 times higher than white families in poverty.

Blacks do not fare much better in the area of education. In 1984, in families where the head had four years of high school, Blacks were 25.5 percent of those in poverty and whites were 7.5 percent. In families where the head had one or more years of college, Blacks were 15.6 percent and whites were 3.9 percent of those in poverty. Cross concludes: "The black/white income deficit that prevails when blacks have equal or better education is powerful evidence that the low educational attainments of blacks do not explain the poverty gap."[9]

Poverty and racism are linked. The elimination of one is intertwined with the elimination of the other.

THE FEMINIZATION OF POVERTY

In the life experiences of Black Americans, the peculiar marriage of racism and poverty was not voluntary. It was arranged, even forced.

In this section, I shall explore the feminization of poverty as put forth in feminist discussions. Discussions on the racialization of poverty begin with the proposition that Black people and other minority peoples bear the brunt of poverty in this country; the feminization of poverty posits that overwhelmingly it is women who bear the burden of poverty. In fact, women and children are the first and most numerous victims.

In 1978, sociologist Diana Pearce coined the phrase "the feminization of poverty" in order to draw attention to the peculiar characteristics of women's poverty that are distinguishable from those of men's poverty. Ruth Sidel observes in *Women and Children Last* that the feminization of poverty resulted from an earlier convergence of social and economic factors. The phenomena that contribute to the increasing impoverishment of women and children include

the weakening of the traditional nuclear family; the rapid growth of female-headed families; the continuing existence of a dual labor market that actively discriminates against female workers; a welfare system that seeks to maintain its recipients below the poverty line; the time-consuming yet unpaid domestic responsibilities of women, particularly child care; and an administration in power in Washington that is systematically dismantling or reducing funds for programs that serve those who are most in need . . . the unemployed; continuing discrimination on the basis of race, class and age; and the changing nature of the economy.[10]

These factors are complicated by the fact that many women early in their lives buy into the notion that they will someday be taken care of by a man, that they do not really need to prepare themselves to be fully independent.[11] In fact, we could argue that because women are taught and socialized into dependency, women's independence is neither encouraged nor rewarded. Immediately after the period when by most accounts the poverty rates fell (the 1960s and 1970s), the Reagan administration nullified the decline and actually contributed to an increase in the level of poverty for women and children. While poverty in families headed by men declined by 50 percent, poverty in families headed by women increased 54 percent.[12] In the early seventies the statistics for Hispanic women and Black women exceeded those percentages.

Another important reason for the feminization of poverty is the dual labor market. Occupational segregation, sex discrimination, and racism still combine to limit women's income and economic mobility. A study conducted by the *Atlanta Journal and Constitution* revealed that women are essentially relegated to nursing, teaching, service, and clerical positions.[13] For the most part, women can at best aspire to be a secondary authority or assistant to a top person. They are often nurses and less often doctors; they are almost exclusively secretaries and less often CEOs. The study found that even in occupations heavily populated by women, leadership is more often male. For example, the public school system has a predominantly female teaching staff and predominantly male leadership (as principals). The study demonstrated further that when women take over previously male occupations, significance or prestige decreases. Conversely, when men take over what are traditionally women's occupations, power and prestige increases. Female cooks are cooks; male cooks are chefs. When women do "men's work" they are sometimes paid less; when men do "women's work" they are often paid more.

Though this study was done in the secular sphere, direct correlations can be made in the church. Here, women are relegated to clerical work, assistantships, and leadership positions in women's auxiliaries, but seldom attain a head pastor's role. Women are often paid less than men in similar positions. When women are called as pastors, they are often paid less than and given smaller churches than men. It seems that in the church as well as in the larger society, the value of women's work is considerably less than that of men's.

SIGNS OF POVERTY

Greg Duncan quotes Leviticus 27:1–4 (as does Sidel), acknowledging that in biblical times (and regrettably in modern times, too) a woman's worth was only three-fifths that of a man's. The U.S. Department of Labor 1973 census figures bear this out. "The ratio of average hourly earnings of women to men was .63 in 1949, .65 in 1959, and .63 in 1969."[14] More specifically, Sidel maintains that women routinely earn less than men.

> *They work in professional fields dominated by men such as accounting, in which female workers comprise less than 40 percent of all workers and earn only 71.2 percent of what men earn; or in retail, in which women make up over 60 percent of the work force and yet earn only 67.4 percent of what men earn; or in occupations dominated by women, such as clerical and kindred jobs, in which women make up 78.4 percent of the work force and yet earn only 67 percent of what men earn.*[15]

According to Sidel, the median income for women in 1983 was $6,320; for men it was $14,630.[16] Clearly, women consistently are financially weaker and therefore more vulnerable than men to a whole array of social threats. The face of poverty is most often feminine. Racial differentials yield even lower wages for Black men, Black women, and other minorities.

LINGERING QUESTIONS

What can we say about these statistics and the questions they beg? What are the bases for them? Why is poverty disproportionately Black and female? It is clear that in North America, to be Black is to have a great likelihood of poverty. Harrington argues that because of "the historic and institutionalized consequence of color . . . being born a Negro will continue to be the most profound disability that the U.S. imposes upon a citizen."[17]

Recognizing the racialization of poverty enables us to examine more completely the Black reality. What we find is that North American culture perpetuates a racial assault on Black men and women and renders them victims of poverty. We are able to see the particular detrimental effects racism has on the Black male in a white patriarchal society in which white manhood is the central reference category (distorted and oppressive though the concept may be).

In a racist society, Black men cannot be "real" men and Black women cannot be "real" women. They are at best facsimiles of manhood and womanhood. When persons are Black and imprisoned by poverty, they are removed even further from the possibilities of being accepted as real human beings.

Just as the racialization of poverty is detrimental to the human dignity of Blacks, the feminization of poverty is detrimental to the dignity of women. Though women are essential to our national life and economy, the sexism reflected in poverty means that women must forever be seen as appendages of men. Because much of women's poverty is directly related to how they are defined in patriarchal structures, they are offered "protective poverty," a kind of protective custody that effectively keeps them "in their place" yet offers only a limited amount of patriarchal protection. It should be noted, however, that Black women have never benefited as white women have from such patriarchal protection.

Analyses of the feminization of poverty have been criticized for their lack of attention to race, a type of racism.[18] In fact, the experience of poverty has always been far worse for Black women than for women of the dominant culture. In *Regulating the Lives of Women,* Mimi Abramovitz recounts the development of welfare policies in America.[19] The Social Security Act was preceded by a pension to widows with young children, reserved primarily for white women. In the 1930s Aid to Dependent Children was established. At this time the state began to regulate female-headed households, insisting that mothers stay home to rear children. However, this patriarchal model was not applied to whites and Blacks alike. The system was designed to ensure that enough Black females were kept out of the programs to provide low-paid domestic help for white families. Black women as a category were described as "undeserving women." It was thought that Black women did, could, and should work, even though the jobs provided for them were inadequate to keep them above the poverty level.[20] All of this indicates that the method for the analysis of poverty and the strategy for its elimination must move beyond sexism and sexist structure to include issues of race.

The theological question is twofold: (1) What kind of God permits the vast "povertization" of women and children? and (2) What is there about the God of white theology that permits the kind of racialized feminization or the feminized racialization of poverty that keeps Blacks and other Third World people, especially women, at the bottom of the social, economic, and political ladder? These questions direct me to a theological challenge and the theological claim for human dignity.

THE THEOLOGICAL MANDATE

As a theologian of the church and an active member of a church, I am impelled to ask why these conditions are allowed to exist. Do they exist because of divine will or because of human will? The pie-in-the-sky theology of old was designed keep people focused upon the other world rather than upon this one.

Some church folks present their sexist, racist, or other worldly theology as though it were normative. They would admonish the poor to look to the skies or to some spiritual fault within themselves rather than to their existential reality in their social context. Christians must ask, has the church become overly spiritualized? Has the contemporary evangelical church lost touch with the radical dimensions of the historical Black church? When African-Americans sang "Steal away to Jesus" or "Onward Christian Soldiers," they were not limited to an eschatological interpretation of their religiosity. They sang of freedom here and now.

When the poor are directed to the skies, they are simply being tricked into doing what Desmond Tutu recounted of the African church's acquiescence to over-spiritualization. The colonizers, Tutu said, brought their Bible to Africa and said, "Let us pray"; the people closed their eyes and bowed their heads, and when they lifted them again, the Europeans had left their Bibles and taken the land. What makes this and similar realities (such as historic slavery in the U.S.A. and apartheid in South Africa) so appalling is that theologians of dominant groups have attempted to justify theologically the colonization and victimization of peoples outside their group, viz., native peoples, Hispanics, African-Americans, Asian-Americans. Moses and Jesus' observation that the poor shall be with us always says more about the nature of fallen humanity than about predetermined characteristics of any group of persons. Surely God could not possibly have ordained or condoned such atrocious racist, sexist, and classist structures that render so many persons permanently poor.

Some years ago, at a conference on the Jeremiah text "Seeking the Welfare of the City," I was scheduled to speak after a major, white, male theological educator whose interpretation of the text led him to a passionate exposition of his theory that the poor are a gift to the middle class. The task of the middle class, he said, is to accept the Christian challenge to respond to the needs of the poor in the city. As he continued I became increasingly uncomfortable, so much so that I could not present the paper I had brought to the conference. Perhaps I was experiencing what many Spirit-sensitive preachers feel when they claim to have an irruption of the Spirit that impresses upon them a last-minute change in their sermon.

As I set my text aside I indicated that I saw no problem with the challenge provided for the Christian bourgeoisie. The problem rested with the theology that informed the challenge.

What does it imply about God to say that God has provided the poor—predominantly Black persons—as a sacrificial gift to the relatively rich—predominantly white persons—in order to teach them to be charitable? How do the poor feel about the "privilege" of being an involuntary sacrificial gift? Can they really appreciate this function? Would white, middle-class people be willing to be so considered? In other words, are they willing to trade places with the poor?

In light of the implicit racist and classist theology that appears to be informing the challenge, perhaps it would be better to advocate a theology of trading places with the poor. Because white, middle-class people are not rushing to trade places so that they could enjoy what it means to be such a gift, the legitimacy of the gift is questionable, to say the least. The proposal is merely an exercise in guilt reduction.

If God is the sovereign God who is against sin, it would be incumbent upon Christians to make the eradication of every sin their highest priority. Oppression destroys human dignity. It reduces human beings to objects. It violates their very personhood. Oppression makes a mockery of peace and justice. Oppression is sin that contradicts the righteousness of God and the dignity of all humanity.

The womanist theological mandate is that we must strive to restore the basic dignity of all creation. To do so, Christians must relinquish their theologies of domination by which some maintain control of women, the poor, and the stranger. Additionally, Christians must relinquish their theologies of charity where the poor are given enough to lessen the guilt of the middle class but not enough to strengthen themselves for the long fight against the culture of poverty. Most of all, Christians must relinquish theologies of domination and submission that uphold a white Father God who dominates nonwhites and nonmales, thus ensuring both the racialization and the feminization of poverty.

Then can come power from the underside of history and "herstory." It is possible that we could begin to experience and view God differently. There is an African ancestral belief that God comes to earth each time a woman is born.[21] Obviously, many theologians and many denominations do not recognize these births. For with the continuous existence of racism, sexism, and classism, the divinity in these births is regularly aborted or murdered after birth by patriarchal gods.

These gods continue to provide the basis for some men to relegate "women's work" to white and Black women, many of whom are then driven to find acceptance in the traditionally African apotheosis of nature. Historically, African-American women have lived a controlled existence that has been so debilitating and disenfranchising that the divine in nature is the only mutually affirming reality. Angelou's poem reminds us that the sun, the moon, the stars, the rain, and the mountains are, finally, all that many women can call their own. In a similar vein, Walker writes, "Dear God. Dear stars, dear trees, dear sky, dear people. Dear Everything, Dear God."[22]

Womanist theology challenges the racialization and the feminization of poverty and directs us to affirm that which is truly liberating—the God who frees us from racism, classism, and all that would sunder creation.

NOTES

1. Alice Walker, *The Color Purple* (New York: Harcourt Brace and Jovanovich, 1983), 242.
2. Ibid., 244.
3. Maya Angelou, "Woman Work," in *And Still I Rise* (New York: Random House, 1978), 31–32.

4. Michael Harrington, *The Other American: Poverty in the United States* (1962; reprint, New York: Harper and Row, 1974), 75.
5. Ibid. Harrington gives as the reasons for fear and lack of confidence the double indignity of racial discrimination and economic oppression resulting in fear, hope, hate, and love.
6. Ibid.
7. Theodore Cross, *The Black Power Imperative* (New York: Faulkner Books, 1986), 225.
8. Ibid.
9. Ibid., 299.
10. Ruth Sidel, *Women and Children Last: The Plight of the Poor Woman in Affluent America* (New York: Penguin Books, 1986), 15.
11. Ibid.
12. Ibid., 15–16.
13. Gayle White, "Women's Work," *Atlanta Constitution,* 31 January 1981. The study was reported in seven parts from 31 January to 6 February 1981.
14. Greg Duncan, *Years of Poverty, Years of Plenty* (Ann Arbor: University of Michigan, Institute for Social Research, 1984), 153.
15. Sidel, *Women and Children,* 66.
16. Ibid.
17. Harrington, *Other American,* 76.
18. For a critique of the feminization of poverty, see Linda Burham, "Has Poverty Been Feminized in Black America?" *Black Scholar* 16 (March/April 1985): 14–24.
19. Mimi Abramovitz, *Regulating the Lives of Women: Social Welfare Policy from Colonial Time to the Present* (Boston: South End Press, 1989). See especially the introduction and chapter 10.
20. An economic analysis of domestic servanthood, an area overwhelmingly Black and female, would demonstrate how the intertwining of racism and sexism works against the empowerment of Black women. For a discussion of this subject, see David Katzman, *Seven Days a Week: Women and Domestic Service in Industrializing America* (New York: Oxford University Press, 1978).
21. Cynthia M. Garnet, "Look at the Sun—See the Truth," *African Commentary* (August 1990): 10.
22. Walker, *The Color Purple,* 242.

4

Confessions of an Academic Liberationist: Riding the Tiger of Liberation

Ronald Goetz

Little Piece of Action, etching

Only a few of the liberation movements of the twentieth century actually use the term "liberation," such as in "liberation theology" or "women's liberation." Labels notwithstanding, I suggest that the dominant characteristic of American philosophical, theological, and ideological discourse in this century has been in one sense or another liberationist, i.e., an attempt to set individuals, classes, races, or genders free from bondage.

To be sure, the diagnoses of the agent of bondage differ wildly. For Freud, the diagnosis is the unresolved Oedipal complex. For Marx, it is the exploitive greed of the capitalist oligarchy. For liberals such as John Stuart Mill, as radically represented by the ACLU, it is every attempt of the majority to stifle the free expression of the individual in purely personal, socially benign pleasures. For anthropologists such as Margaret Mead and the cultural relativism she represents, it is the failure to recognize that there are no morally transcendent rights or wrongs—that all taboos, perhaps particularly sexual taboos and ethical codes, are merely the arbitrary mores of particular cultures. For American pragmatists such as John Dewey, it is a conservative orientation to the rigid dogmas of the past, namely, that "truth" is the ever-progressive process of discovery that is functionally determined. Truth is that which works; there is no other truth. For many existentialists, even the fluid, operational truth of the pragmatist is a confining delusion. Indeed, there is no truth. Life is absurd. Or existence, as the more recent fashion has it, is a basking in utter indeterminacy of all meaning. Thus, liberation is a luminescent affirmation of the utter meaninglessness of all meaning. For disciples of Malcolm X, the focus of all bondage is racism. For feminists, the oppression of women is the even earlier and perhaps deeper wrong.

Many of these diagnoses, as well as their accompanying remedies, are in tension with one another and tend to cancel each other out. Liberation can hardly be achieved through a society that features both Marxist collectivism and Millian individualism. The failure of communism in Eastern Europe demonstrates that the two are a drastic either/or. Freud would liberate by enabling us to be resigned to the profound and utter darkness of the human psyche and the tragedy of human existence; however, this is hardly of a piece with Mead's fiction of the idealized primitive effervescently copulating his or her way into the Reign of Heaven on earth. The pragmatists would liberate us from the past by showing us the way to open-minded, democratic, practical problem-solving; yet there are many in the humanities departments of our universities who would offer liberation through the quasinihilistic exposure of the falsehood of every claim of so-called open-mindedness or so-called solutions. On the racial and gender fronts, I feel safe in assuming that even if she were not disqualified by her race, Gloria Steinem would not feel particularly comfortable accepting the liberated woman's role as it is defined in Louis Farrakahn's Nation of Islam.

Our nation was founded in a revolution fueled by the eighteenth-century Enlightenment belief in the inevitable progress of humanity. Europe, still our main cultural wellspring, is perhaps more circumspect concerning progress. But *we* are future-oriented. For us the past exists in order to be improved upon. Our belief in progress overrides specific political agendas.

For example, in 1980 the American people were not Reaganites in terms of many of Reagan's specific proposals. Apart from Jimmy Carter's foreign-policy problems and his seeming lack of consistent resolve, Carter's vision of conservationist, "small is beautiful" America all but guaranteed Reagan's victory. That the next generation may not live in greater plenty than our own, that the upward spiral of material wealth might have to be permanently governed for the sake of the environment and the poor, was a way of thinking so out of touch with the American dream that Carter was radically unelectable.

Of course, most of the intellectual community saw through Reagan's empty rhetoric. His vision of wealth for the wealthy now (by means of subversive tax cuts), of vast trade imbalances and catastrophic indebtedness, did not fool everybody. Not only did Reagan seem a buffoon to many intellectuals, but the intellectual community had its own far more profound diagnosis and far more radical solutions.

Nevertheless, despite the conflicts between the American intellectual establishment and the anti-intellectual Reaganites, we all drink from some of the same spiritual wells. Americans simply cannot think for long apart from the myth of progress and the primacy of the individual. The progress of the nation measured by the happiness of individuals is our destiny. The only remaining questions, and to be sure they are significant ones, are the following: What constitutes happiness, and how is our progress toward it to be achieved? Do we follow Deweyite reform and the amelioration of social ills by open-minded, scientific, democratic, rational solution, i.e., the way liberal Democrats claim to follow? Or perhaps by revolution: Marxist or racial or feminist, etc.? Or as Reagan sought to achieve progress—through voodoo economics?

Along with these impressionistic background remarks I want to make my own confession: I am a left-leaning liberationist. No matter how I despair of the continued integrity of the left, I would have to break with all the sentiments of my youth and middle years in order to link arms with reactionaries. I agree with Karl Barth's aphorism that the radical is probably wrong but has a chance of being right; the conservative is always wrong.

I have a good leftist liberationist pedigree. In 1951, when Joe McCarthy was terrorizing the country, I was a freshman at Northwestern University, a then, as now, very conservative institution. I was a socialist, a member of Northwestern's tiny Progressive Students Association. Some of my friends were communists, although I could never make that move. A number of my friends were homosexual, and though I definitely could not make *that* move, I was an advocate of gay liberation long before the slogan was invented. My father had insisted I join ROTC, but at the time I was expected to accept the commission, I refused on pacifist grounds.

In my youth, my greatest passion was jazz and most of my cultural heroes were Black. From my high-school days on, I regarded racism and Jim Crow laws as a kind of blasphemy. I have always opposed censorship. Long before it was fashionable, I helped with housework and tended the kids—and now the grandkids. My wife and daughters, who would know, claim to see no significant hint of sexism in me. I was against our country's involvement in Vietnam from the beginning. I support the ecological movement, contribute to Jacques Cousteau and Greenpeace, and admire Ralph Nader. In short, my liberal heart bleeds a torrent. I may no longer be able to make much sense of a doctrinaire socialism, but I am at least as far to the left as Ted Kennedy, except in terms of his liberated sexual adventuring.

Given the fact that none of us is utterly consistent, and that our perspectives evolve, I admit to having dipped my hands in many of the movements to which I have alluded. I have read Marx and Freud. But I have always believed in freedom and I have always had a streak of individualism—some of it Millian, some of it Kierkegaardian.

Americans do not much care that the various modern liberationists' ideals often cancel out one another. We tend to be intellectually eclectic. Radical ideological, philosophical, or theological consistency has never been the American way. Further, a dogged consistency fares poorly in a culture such as ours that is so susceptible to fads and fashions. The consistent ideologue is inevitably left holding the bag. The shrewd American intellectual always leaves a path of retreat from absolute answers, lest he or she be caught advocating last year's truths.

However, beyond the matter of fashion, we subordinate all ideology to the strongest impulses of our souls, an ad hoc amalgam of progressive individualism and utilitarian practicality. We tend to distrust collectivism or overly consistent thought systems that would interpret all reality through a single prism. If I read modern intellectual history correctly, therefore, when we make use of such deterministic or collectivistic schemas as Marxism or Freudianism or even feminism, we do so as Americans; that is, we put all such ideologies in the service of the far more basic American impulse toward an individualistically defined sense of progress and pragmatic utility.

The leftist liberationist reads Marx because Marx is useful in what is finally an individualistically motivated assault upon those aspects of the establishment that the liberationist judges to be inhibiting. Despite the continued fashionableness of Marxism, comparatively few current American intellectuals would ever countenance the surrender of their personal liberties in order to live in a Marxist collective. Freud is a useful tool in the modern campaign against traditional sexual mores or belief in a God who makes requirements and who judges, but few would buy into the dark determinism of the Freudian system. We take any intellectual tool at hand, often irrespective of its implications, and use it in our disparately conceived struggles for liberty.

I am not claiming that there is no altruism in our liberation impulses. This would be rankly cynical. Indeed, though our love of liberty takes a radically individualistic turn, we are, as nations go, remarkably altruistic. Every news account of individual misfortune brings outpourings of money and goodwill. However, the generosity we express toward individuals and the emergency aid we send to other nations in times of natural disasters too rarely move us to go on to support sustained and costly programs to eradicate suffering on a long-term, systematic basis.

No model of liberation has the self-evident, objective, scientific status that is often claimed. Rather than being a disinterested, universally valid appraisal, each liberation model reflects the individuality and the social situation of the one who conceives it. My needs and interests, my class and race influence my sense of injustice and justice, my insights and prejudices, what I think I know and what is actually the case, what I believe would serve to liberate me and mine and perhaps the rest of humanity. I can certainly be wrong, even about my own liberation, and I can choose a path of so-called liberation that actually enslaves me as an individual or enslaves whole populations, as communism's true believers have so painfully learned. However, even when I am able to discern the course that would seem to be individually liberating, there is no guarantee that the paths to *my* liberation will help people of other races and other socioeconomic situations. What puts the prosperous at liberty may prove poison to the poor.

The mainline American churches of the twentieth century have radically introduced one species or another of liberation as the essence of Christian ethics. Reinhold Niebuhr, this century's most influential Christian ethicist, brought a hard-nosed Marxist analysis to the social gospel tradition and radically focused upon political/social/economic liberation. His brother, H. Richard Niebuhr, feared that he went so far as to reduce the providential purpose of God to the achievement of the liberal political agenda. To be sure, Reinhold Niebuhr was too much a lutheran (I emphasize the small *l*) and too much of a Marxist to be viewed as a stereotypical individualist. While he was clearly no anthill collectivist, Niebuhr's whole sense of Christian responsibility centered in his vision of political relevancy. Perhaps his greatest thinking was in terms of strategies to achieve social justice—for example, he presaged the whole strategy of Martin Luther King and the SCLC as early as 1932.[1]

Reinhold Niebuhr's dark sense of the brokenness of the human condition and the impossibility of moral progress might at first glance make it seem improbable that he should achieve the eminence he did in optimistic America. However, his political thinking finally resolved itself in an almost Deweyite pragmatism.[2] With Dewey, Niebuhr saw that utopian perfection, grand schemes, and final solutions are delusions. Nevertheless, within the democratic system, by political pressure, rational calculation, and goodwill, we can achieve *proximate* justice. For Niebuhr, the highest goal of Christian social ethics lay not in some spurious utopian attempt to achieve the Reign of God on earth but in the effort to achieve a partial but significant amelioration of social ills and relative social progress. Christianity must make its vision of love relevant at the larger social level or such love is ultimately irrelevant to humanity. Niebuhr had some shrewd and wise things to say on matters of personal ethics, but they were occasional to his larger agenda—social liberation.

Many secular enthusiasts found Niebuhr's ethics detachable from his theological convictions—there were many "atheists for Niebuhr," as they called themselves. His ambivalence toward belief in life beyond the grave, his language about God as a "symbol" so that one might wonder if Godtalk has any objective cash value beyond its references to the forces of history, make such atheistic enthusiasm understandable— although it fails to grasp the full Niebuhr, who was, secularity notwithstanding, Niebuhr the Christian.

Paul Tillich was Niebuhr's colleague and the inheritor of his mantle as the lion of American theology, the last such lion this country has seen. Tillich, whose Godtalk was, if anything, even more ambiguous than Niebuhr's, taught an ethic of personal fulfillment. One is ethically responsible to develop one's self as a total being—creatively, spiritually, and sensually. Shaped by twentieth-century existentialism, Tillich was deeply affected by the ambiguities and paradoxes of life, and he was profoundly alienated from religious, metaphysical, and social orthodoxy. He reflected the liberationist themes of the early twentieth-century avant-garde of his native Germany, with its revolutionary expressionism, its revolutionary Marxism, and perhaps above all, its fascination with Nietzsche and his contempt for the enslaving constraints of conventional bourgeois morality.

Because of the elusive character of Tillich's discourse, few of his students discerned that his ethical impulse toward personal fulfillment was compatible in his mind with compulsive womanizing. However, when this was posthumously disclosed by his wife, Hanna, one could see that the hints were there in his theology. Perhaps it should not have been utterly surprising that Tillich carried his liberating program of self-fulfillment against the constraints of convention to the extreme of sexual license.[3]

The modern mainline churches have always been adept at sniffing the wind. It is therefore to be expected that liberation in all its ambiguity should be one of the few dogmas to unite the leadership of an otherwise chaotic organization. Thus, while the average person might think that mainline churches would be a remaining bastion of "family values" such as abhorrence of easy divorce and strong advocacy of marital fidelity and sacrificial commitment in the bearing and raising of children, etc., in fact, much of the theological ethics done in the seminaries is as liberated as the most worldly secularism. For many, sexual deprivation is a greater evil than uninhibited fornication. Divorce is commonplace. Abortion is the bulwark on which family planning and women's liberation is built.[4] Tillich was not an aberration; he was a prophet of the church's liberated sexuality.

Niebuhr came to despise Tillich for his lifestyle.[5] I think it would have caused him grief to see his call for a worldly Christian social responsibility fused with Tillich's ethic of worldly self-fulfillment. But many in the church have achieved just such an amalgam. Liberals both inside and out of the church take a rather self-righteous pride in separating an individual's social/political stance from his or her sexual lifestyle. (That is, perhaps, unless a person is celibate—then it is safe to suggest that something is wrong with him or her.)

When personal rectitude is seen as irrelevant to political/social rectitude we see individualism gone mad. Further, such a double standard lets the general public off the hook on social/political issues. They despise not just the messenger but the message itself when someone's private life is a contradiction of his or her public positions, as in the case of the womanizing politician who advocates women's rights. How easy it is to dismiss the moral seriousness of such political positions.

It would be cavalier to suggest that poverty is a state of mind, but it is true that poor people's sense of their poverty is determined by their comparative status in the larger society. Many a welfare family has far more creature comforts (electricity, central heating, television, etc.), far more effective medical care, better public sanitation, and better basic nutrition than did the family of a well-off medieval burgher, and the average American welfare family would be a model of prosperity to most families in Ethiopia today. This is not to suggest that relative American poverty is excusable because Ethiopian poverty is worse. It is merely to say that "poor" is in many ways a relative term. Each society teaches its poor that they are poor, and it also models to them what it is to be successful. It is in the modeling of liberated success in America that the haves can be so destructive to the have nots.

Few are naive enough to expect politicians to model much more than American venality. So where does the American dream get modeled to the poor? Television ads equate success with sexiness and possessions, with the constant suggestion that the latter two convey the former. Many stars of the entertainment world flaunt the libertine self-indulgences permitted to society's idols. Talk shows endlessly transmit the vulgar, individualistically liberated pluralistic, relativistic, self-permissive claptrap that dominates the more "sophisticated" deliberations of the intellectual elite. It is no longer fashionable to predict the outright disappearance of the nuclear family, but few are coming to terms with the duty, responsibility, and steadfastness without which family life, not to say the rearing of mentally and spiritually able offspring, is impossible. The Black middle class understandably flees the dangerous inner-city ghettos, where pimps, whores, and drug dealers are often the only models of success young people encounter firsthand.

Financial resources can cushion and mask some of the long-term havoc that our post-liberation ethical situation creates for the middle and upper classes and their children. However, when the poor see respectable success modeled as liberation from moral self-discipline and a commitment to duty beyond one's own immediate happiness, there is not enough money to cushion anything. The poor are ultimately confronted with bills they cannot pay when they seek to emulate the utter liberation of the elite.

This says nothing of the personal grief, such as broken marriages and emotionally scarred children, that the erosion of bourgeois morality often causes the bourgeoisie themselves, irrespective of their wealth. One can only wonder with deep misgivings how the health of the nation will be affected by such a liberated phenomenon as the trend toward one-parent families, not just among the poor but in the middle and upper classes as well.

When the intellectual elite of the Christian church become fashionably liberated in their sexual attitudes and activities, they claim as dualists that because their enlightened spirits are liberated from lust what they do with their bodies is unimportant (ironically, though dualism has become a dirty word, they resemble the more decadent among the ancient gnostics). Is there not a hint of intellectual gnostic egotism in the implicit claim that the wisdom and insight one contributes with one's intellect renders irrelevant the activities of one's glands?

Of course, our sexuality is a great gift. Clearly, it is no evil if we, impelled by our natures as sexual beings, invest a great deal in our sexuality. Nevertheless, the very power of the sex drive can leave us blinded by desire to duty. We can easily forget that our sexuality is intended to build relationships, not corrupt them, that it is intended to help us keep our promises to others, not to stimulate disloyalty.

Sexuality can serve, as Paul Lehmann put it, as a parental bulwark against the tyranny of children; i.e., the sex act makes us more than just biological parents. It can give us intense moments of mutual sharing that help us to cope with the burdens of parenthood and thus be better, more loving parents. But the sex drive can also be perverted into incest. As I hear it, theological discourse on sex has for years focused on sexual freedom, above all freedom from guilt, and in such a way that sexual freedom is implicitly placed at odds with Christian sexual responsibility.

Many pastors who are on the front lines in the sexual revolution, and who are expected by their congregations to uphold marital fidelity, are themselves torn between the liberated norms of the larger society, the demands of their consciences as Christians, and the demands of their congregations. The theology and the role modeling prospective pastors find in seminaries are not doing much to strengthen their resolve to marital fidelity. Nor are they helping them find the way to a new sexual morality in the light of radical changes in modern sexual consciousness that would both accord with the Christian gospel and bear the light of public scrutiny. In this struggle they are left largely to their own devices.

My point is not to incite some moralistic inquisition in seminaries or among pastors. It is simply to point out that the cultural torrent of sexual liberation into which the mainline church has so deeply immersed itself makes that church, progressive protestations notwithstanding, irrelevant to many of the problems afflicting the poor. Many of the American poor suffer not just from a lack of funds, but also from the tragic moral deprivation that occurs when there is a fundamental breakdown of monogamy and the two-parent family. The Yuppie myth, that quality time makes up for and indeed is better than more constant parental attention, is increasingly being exploded as we are seeing more and more children being negatively impacted by the experiment.

However, when the children of poverty are raised in single-parent families, which are deprived of the vital nurturing that ideally requires the energies and role modeling of both parents, the impact of pecuniary and cultural deprivation upon the children is often devastating. Children in dysfunctional families experience a tragic loss of self-esteem; thus, there is little bulwark against the lure of urban crime, and little compensation for the breakdown in many educational systems. In the case of minorities, there is little to strengthen the child in the face of racism. What results is the perpetuation of the cycle of defeatism.

At the very moment when the two-parent family is on the decline, particularly among Blacks,[6] the liberationist elite in the church have either been raised to a higher level of gnostic liberty and self-fulfillment or long ago intellectually succumbed to modern, permissive relativizing and thereby forfeited the right or the conviction to speak convincingly and by example about familial duty, faithfulness, and self-sacrifice.

No theological contortions, however dexterous, can disguise the fact that well-off Christians who indulge themselves in our general cultural "liberation" make themselves the enemies of the very familial commitments without which the children of the poor in America can never rise. Of course, we need a genuine, massive, sustained governmental war on poverty. But without strong families the benefits of such programs will always be stunted. The state cannot instill values and self-esteem in children. The state can only provide a level playing field.

I am not calling for a return to the good old days—the days when the stigma against divorce led to interminable, loveless, debilitating marriages; when puberty was greeted with guilt and nonsense about endless exercise, cold showers, and insanity or blindness brought on by masturbation; when family planning was the work of the devil or, even worse, an assault on Aristotle as the infallible teacher of Christian ethics.

The good old answers to social issues have no more to commend them. The good old answer to child delinquency was child labor. The good old answer to the uppity Negro was the strange fruit that hung on southern trees. The good old answer to unemployment was the sweatshop or the wage slavery of the company town. The good old answer to frankness was censorship. The good old answer to national adventurism was knee-jerk patriotism or jail. The good old answer of many churches to economic exploitation, racism, and sexism was pious submission that supposedly would imitate the suffering of Jesus. The good days are well gone, and in a culture in which we have tasted more liberties than at any time in human history, the notion that we *could* return to Victorian mores is an illusion.

Still, many of us are sickened by some of the license we have set free: flagrant pornography, millionaire rock stars howling for the brutalization of women or the suicide of their fans, the epidemic of drug use. We get angry over the impunity with which crimes are committed, and we may be dismayed by the miscarriages of justice created by such things as the exclusionary rule of law (though God help the innocent if the new Supreme Court undoes the exclusion of illegally gathered evidence). Perhaps we sometimes even wonder if we have more liberty than most of us wish to live with, but see no alternatives. We are riding the tiger of liberation, and while we may often enjoy the ride, we are clearly afraid to get off.

Yet despite our culture's heady if perilous progress in personal, individual liberty, the poor remain dispossessed. Liberationists from the right and from the left have waged war upon oppression and upon each other (even the gun lobby uses liberationist rhetoric to great effect). The result is that liberty that was once won at a great cost now comes by default. Few have the energy or the conviction to say no once they have gotten theirs. Thus, liberty abounds at the same time that the poor and particularly the Black poor are on the verge of sinking into a permanent underclass.

To be sure, every welfare mother has the *civil* right to check into an exclusive hotel for a weekend of relaxation away from the kids. Blacks may soon be able to purchase memberships in $35,000-a-year country clubs. There are job openings galore for Black Ph.D.s, sex or sexual orientation notwithstanding. All such fruits of the liberation struggle are largely irrelevant to the situation of the poor.

Despite the best intentions and rhetoric of the leftist liberationist elite, among whom I clearly count myself, liberation has come to the poor on a trickle-down basis. When the Reaganites boasted of being trickle-down benefactors, we on the left despised them for their elitist contempt of the poor. But despite our high-sounding sentiments, what have we who are educated, who are not poor, accomplished? A cynic might say that we have made good livings and salved our consciences by spouting loftily about freedom and justice while the poor continue to grow in number, many of them so damaged by deprivation that they seem irrevocably estranged from the mainstream.

Howard K. Smith, now retired from television newscasting, was interviewed some months ago on public T.V. He had a number of wise things to say, but above all, he put his finger on the truth of the American political mood. Commenting on George Bush's inaugural address, in which he said that the American people have the will to resolve the nation's great social problems but not the resources, Smith observed that the exact opposite was in fact the case. We are still the richest nation on earth, and we have abundant resources to do whatever cries out to be done, but we do not have the will to do it. The issue confronting us in the light of poverty in America is not at the deepest level a political, sociological, economic, or bureaucratic problem. Beneath all these "technical" issues, we confront a profound national moral malaise.

We need to speak of such things as moral failure and moral guilt. While no one has a monopoly on moral failure, clearly the primal and greatest fault lies in the callousness of those of us who have the power and wealth in society. The responsibility of the poor for the exacerbation of their own misery—by the epidemics of crime, drug use, absentee fathers and husbands, and out-of-wedlock births—can be discussed only secondarily, and never to mitigate the prior guilt of America's ruling elite.

Reinhold Niebuhr in the 1930s preached a sermon on the labor movement in which he took his text from the apostle Paul: "We have a righteousness not our own." Labor has a righteousness not its own, Niebuhr said. That is, the cause of labor is more righteous than are the workers themselves. If workers achieved justice and enjoyed the inevitable power that would thus come to the labor movement, labor itself would become a part of the problem, for power corrupts. So, too, one need not mythologize the innocence of the poor in order to affirm the radical rightness of their cause. But the failures of the poor are no justification for the self-righteousness callousness of the rich.

Increasingly the continued intractability of poverty—particularly Black poverty—is the occasion for Americans who have "made it," in self-serving despair to claim that responsibility for poverty in America lies with the poor themselves. We, the relatively affluent, mitigate our culpability in the perpetuation of poverty.

The nuts and bolts of what to do about poverty are difficult enough. These are matters that the intellectual establishment is equipped to help society solve. However, practical proposals are irrelevant if we have not faced the question of ethical resolve. There can be no addressing the problem of American poverty, to say nothing of the far more difficult problem of world poverty, without affirming that national sacrifice ought to be our chief moral imperative. The need for a more progressive tax system is a given. But beyond this, we must recognize that the obligation of Americans to commit themselves to more modest lifestyles is as compelling as our obligation to refrain from committing murder and theft.

There is no morally justifiable excuse for poverty in America. We could radically turn the corner on poverty in a decade if we had the moral will to do so. But where is the moral leadership to come from?

In the highest corridors of academe most of us have long ago lost the capacity to speak with a compelling moral voice. Some of us even boast that the only real knowledge is value-free knowledge. Certainly my field, theology, where the naive soul might expect to find some last holdout for radical moral and religious commitment, is no exception. Increasingly, our subject matter is not God, revelation, redemption; it is not ethics, not even theological anthropology. Rather, the subject of theology has become theology itself. Much theology has dissolved into a narcissistic examination of its own methodology. If only the right methodology can be established, theology might still be able to hang on, despite the general intellectual climate of pluralism, skepticism, relativism, and individualistic liberation. Lurking behind all this is the fear that the utter liberty of a world without norms means the death of God.

The general breakdown of theological confidence or even a collapse of faith in God will not put us theologians out of work, thus swelling the roles of the impoverished. We will always find people to pay us for what we do. However, do not expect much help from us in terms of ethical vision or leadership. The youth of the country have a handle on what's going on in the academe as a whole—academe of which theology is but a microcosm. Surveys taken some twenty years ago showed that more than 80 percent of college-bound students hoped that college would help them develop a philosophy of life. Now less than 20 percent have such hope.

Not only has an utterly relativized educational establishment lost its moral claim to the expectations of many students, but some of our most privileged youth are exhibiting an increasingly jaded cynicism toward the claims of the oppressed. Writing in that bible of academia *Chronicle of Higher Education,* Chester E. Finn, Jr., observes that it has become increasingly apparent, certainly among white males, that "obtaining status, attention, privileges, resources and sundry other advantages, at least within academe, is associated with getting one's group identified as victims."[7] Thus we are seeing white student unions, men's studies programs, and straight pride rallies springing up on a number of campuses. Liberationism has gone from being an albeit divided and pluralistic faith commitment to the liberation of society's victims to a cynical technique by which society's privileged can debilitate all moral appeals by means of such callous reductio ad absurdums. Men's studies programs, indeed![8]

I do not want to suggest that the American intellectualist establishment is universally corrupt. Perhaps I am just pointing out the fact that most of its leading spirits are tenured. A tenured radical borders on something of a contradiction in terms. We have discovered in our liberated democracy that the most effective way to neutralize protest is to co-opt it—to permit everyone to speak freely, indeed, to guarantee the rights of those inclined to insult and malign the system. What results is a Babel of ethical voices. Then we put professors to work studying, decoding, debating with great fervor this Babel, and finally the world yawns. The guarantee of total intellectual freedom has wonderfully served to keep us intellectuals in our places.[9] Despite our staggering technical expertise and our vaunted freedom, today's intelligentsia has produced no compelling moral agenda—this is not what it is paid to do.

This all becomes depressing only if one places final hope in the dreams and schemes of the human race. I love the human race, warts, pimples, and all—and I also love God, the creator of the world over which humanity has dominion, the God who can in his providence make more of our dreams and schemes than we can imagine.

Therefore, we ought never to become too downhearted because we are finite and our rationality can never take account of all things. To be sure, the ecology of existence is such that everything we do reverberates beyond our capacity to control it. We can never escape the irony that sometimes evil things result from the best intentions and sometimes great good comes from the wanton intentions of wicked men and women. Nevertheless, we know that on balance, most people find life in all its ambiguity a greater good than evil. There are few of us who, like Dostoyevski's Ivan Karamazov, would prefer never to have been born.

Certainly, we Christians can never finally despair. How could we, when we have been given to know that it is love that makes the world go 'round? To despair would be to blaspheme the graciousness of God. Despite its brutal realism concerning human frailty, the Bible witnesses to the overriding goodness of human progress through history. Sin notwithstanding, human existence is not in the last analysis evil.

That the evolution of human history is finally to be affirmed rests for the Christian on two fundamental contentions—that the creation is itself good and that God never utterly abandons us to our own devices. We have a faithful and gracious partner working beside us in all our endeavors within this good creation. We are always upheld by the providence of the living God, who does not despise our finite efforts but who redeems them in this world and into eternity.

God's partnership is revealed in many ways. There is in all things God's underlying sustaining of our world—God's subtle and hidden working within the very fiber of being, as God inspires, draws, attracts the good creation toward a blessed end. Clearly, not everything in life is mere sin, not everything is broken. Nevertheless, evil and sin sometimes seem to triumph and the good creation may appear to be inherently fallen. How often God must reign redemptively. That is God reigning through an ex post facto picking up of the pieces of the shambles we have made of the world. Other times God takes a more direct lead by redemptively raising up prophets to declare God's own Word.

To be sure, some prophets are despised in their own time and among their own people, such as Amos or Jeremiah. But a Moses or a Joshua was thrust by the redemptive providence of God into the leadership of God's contentious and often faithless people. No one in his or her right mind would want to be a prophet of any sort. At best, they are able to stay one step ahead of the assassin's blade or bullet. The obedience of the prophet's people is at best partial, and their faithfulness is fleeting.

What we need today is a prophet who can reawaken in us the ancient vision in a way that makes us see how the everlasting word of God is ever new. Perhaps this is too much to ask. Our nation has already in this century had one towering prophet of God—Martin Luther King. Maybe it is not for us to see his like again.

However, we can at least review his central word to us—that racism and social and economic injustice injures the humanity of the oppressor as well as the oppressed, and there can never be a righteous society until both victim and victimizer are healed. King rejected the we/they model of human relations. The we/they model that collects injustices like scalps. The we/they model that encourages the very hostility it seeks to heal. King rejected any ideology that taught that the liberation of one people required the ruin of another.

King refused to cooperate with injustice, and thus he resisted those who did evil. However, he and the civil rights workers who followed him were willing to bear their oppressors' hostility by turning the other cheek. Through such acts of unmerited suffering the oppressors were brought face to face with the evil they were doing. For many whites, the impact of such a Gandhian, Christlike witness was powerful, and for many, it did indeed lead to repentance and healing.

It would be breathtakingly presumptuous of me, a white, middle-class, synthetic sage, to propose to the Blacks in America: Go back to nonviolent resistance, go back to cross-bearing, and you will find the soft heart of white America willing to take you in. Apart from the smug paternalism of such a suggestion, there is the sheer cheek of a member of the ruling class suggesting to the oppressed that they should behave like saints so that their overlords might come to love them.

Because Martin Luther King was a prophet raised up by God, he could say things with an authority that cut through the cynicism that pertains to many human proposals. But even King at the time of his murder found that many of his own people could no longer accept the authority of his call to nonviolent resistance to evil. They rejected his leadership—rather as Miriam and Aaron turned against Moses.

Perhaps we should pray that next time God raises up a prophet or judge among us, it will be a white woman or man. The Blacks, not to say the Native Americans and the Hispanics, have borne the prophetic burden, been struck on the cheek, quite enough. Perhaps it is time for the masters of the universe to turn the other cheek.

A sign of the divine calling of such a prophet would be his or her capacity to articulate a vision of justice and love that proclaims that all sides of the body politic need to be healed, and that we can never be healed unless we are healed together. Of course, such a prophet would speak of the liberation of the nation from the cancer of racism and injustice. Of course, the deliverance of God's people in the Exodus would remain the biblical paradigm for that deliverance. But perhaps such a prophet might warn his or her white brethren that the deliverance of the rulers of our society will not come if they focus merely on the escape of the rabble that was Israel when the big wind blew on the Red Sea. There is infinitely more to freedom than successfully taking it on the lam.

Indeed, what we Americans take to be freedom is often merely a selfish escape from responsibility. The American elite are the most liberated people on earth. But the lifestyle we dignify by calling it "freedom" is costing the poor of the first, second, and third worlds dearly. The true freedom of the elite of our society will not come if we conceive of freedom as escape from the burdens of responsibility. Only when we who are privileged arrive at Sinai, only when we are there chastened for our adoration of the calf of gold, and at Sinai are bound hand and foot by the holy law of God, only then will we begin to taste real freedom.

Despite our vaunted liberty and our ceaseless clamor for further liberation, we are not very free at all, at least in the high sense that Moses envisioned and Jesus Christ promises. The highest freedom is actually antithetical to a footloose liberty. The highest freedom contradicts the naive notion that freedom is the capacity to do anything that one's moods or one's glands dictate. Such is actually an incontinent slavery to whim and fashion. The freedom Christ offers us is freedom from such slavery so that we might be able to do our duty, to do what is merciful and just.

Could it be that the reason we are so cold of heart in the face of the outcry of the poor, both here and abroad, is that we are not free, that we are so enslaved by the liberties, pleasures, possessions, and status of this world that we cannot contemplate life without these things? Could it be that in the end, our quest for ceaseless liberation has brought us not freedom but enslavement to mere things?

NOTES

1. See Reinhold Niebuhr, *Moral Man and Immoral Society* (New York: Charles Scribner and Sons, 1960), 250–54.
2. Though Richard Wightman Fox may somewhat underestimate Niebuhr's theological intentions, he is certainly not wrong in pointing out the irony that Niebuhr was closer to Dewey than Niebuhr's icy, antiliberal rhetoric would even seem to indicate. See Fox's *Reinhold Niebuhr, A Biography*, (New York: Pantheon Books, 1985), 165–66.
3. For an analysis of the relationship between Tillich's theology and his life-

style see Melvin L. Vulgamore, "Tillich's 'Erotic Solution'," in *Encounter* 45 (Summer 1984): 193–212.

After I read this paper to the conference, David Buttrick in personal conversation observed that while he had heard criticism of the flaw in Tillich's theology, exposed through Tillich's sexual activities, voiced before, he had never head a Barthian speak about the flaw in Barth's theology that permitted his virtually polygamous relationship with Charlotte von Kirschbaum. I observed that I was tracing some of the influences on the American mainline church and that I believed Tillich had a greater direct influence in terms of ethics on the thinking of the church than did Barth. However, I would affirm that Barth's sexual behavior was no less reprehensible than Tillich's, or Martin Luther King's for that matter. I went on to argue that Barth's actions were a violation of his own best theology and did not flow from or into his thought, as in the case of Tillich. Buttrick replied that Barth's actions did indeed reveal a flaw in Barth's theology as serious as Tillich's. Buttrick insisted that in Barth's theology there is a fundamental unreality that transfers from his theological posture to the sort of ethical unreality that would allow him to suppose he could move his theological assistant into his home as a kind of second wife. I thanked Buttrick for insisting on the weakness in Barth's theology that such an act exhibits. He is right. Barth's imperious, exclusively theological focus, his isolating himself from the insights of psychology or sociology, led him to sometimes write with a seemingly abstracted detachment from the realities and issues of the world about him. That this would result in the incredibly imperious presumption that he could pull off a blatant affair does indeed cast a shadow on this theology.

Ironically, this same Barth was the most politically active and influential theologian that the German-speaking church has seen in this century. Indeed, he invented the slogan that one must do theology with the Bible in one hand and the newspaper in the other. Therefore, one has every right to demand to know on what principle could Barth decide to attack Hitler, attack the self-righteousness of the West during the Cold War, fight against nuclear weapons, and then turn around and do a theology that not only is anti-apologetic but that can be utterly removed from the challenges of a contemporary culture that demands that its agenda be taken seriously and to which the church is trying to address the gospel of Jesus Christ.

I do not admit to being a Barthian but I have learned much from Barth. I would accept for myself the phrase Buttrick used concerning himself: post-Barthian. As a post-Barthian I want to reiterate that not only can

Barth be no more justified in this matter than can Tillich, but indeed, if Barth is the better theologian, his personal lapse is all the more inexcusable. He should have known better.

When Mary Daly issued her broadside against Barth (*Beyond God the Father* (Boston: Beacon Press, 1973), I doubt that she was aware of Barth's relationship with Charlotte. However, Barth's understanding of the relationship between men and women (which despite its moments of great insight does not fundamentally challenge a biblicistic understanding of the male as the first among equals) opens the door to his presumptuous use of the two women in his life. Daly was not always academically fair to Barth, but her instincts on this point were better than I previously recognized.

Despite Barth's frequently self-depreciating humor, he had the self-confidence bordering on arrogance of one who was willing and able to take on the whole theological world. His challenge to the theology of his time bore much fruit. However, as I reflect on the way his arrogance spilled over into his family life, I am a bit more circumspect in rejoicing over his theology. One Barthian I know observed that while Barth's relationship to Charlotte might be regrettable, at least it gave us the dogmatics. If so, the cost was very high. The same must be said about Martin Luther King. Apart from what his philandering must have done to his family and to the women he used, his promiscuity served to discredit the cause that God had forced upon him.

4. Whatever one thinks of abortion, the insistence that it is solely a woman's decision and that her partner has no legal and perhaps no moral stake in it certainly serves to erode the commitment men can be expected to feel toward a child that a woman, answerable only to herself, decides to carry to term. Women's liberation can serve to foster the libertine irresponsibility of men toward children.

5. See Fox, *Reinhold Niebuhr,* 257–59.

6. Not only is the Black divorce rate on a par with the staggeringly high national average, but divorced males' refusal to pay child support, already epidemic among whites, has become almost universal among Black males. Add to this the fact by 1987, 62 percent of Black births were to unmarried mothers, and the percentage seems to be climbing.

7. Chester E. Finn, "Why Can't Colleges Convey Our Diverse Culture's Unifying Themes?" *Chronicle of Higher Education,* 13 June 1990, A40.

8. Classical Marxism assumed that because the proletariat, the victims of capitalism, were the majority, they would secure their own liberation by means of violent revolution. Mao Tse-tung held that justice could be obtained only through the barrel of a gun. However, with the evolution of

capitalism in America, this revolution has been dislocated, because the majority have become middle class. No longer are the majority poor. Further, poverty is disproportionately the lot of many Black Americans, putting them in a double minority status. Even women, though demographically the majority, have no decisive majority power. They are not united in a single agenda; for example, not all women are feminists. In such inherent pluralism, liberation, whether race, gender, or world, cannot be won by an irresistible revolutionary tide. Taking a page from Reinhold Niebuhr or from Martin Luther King in *Why We Can't Wait*, we can observe that successful liberationist movements depend on at least three factors: (1) the rational establishment of the victim status of those seeking liberation; (2) the use of pressure tactics to assure that the cause of the victim is not ignored (it must be made more socially disordering to ignore the aggrieved group than to heed its outcry); and (3) moral persuasion. If the majority cannot be compelled to accept the justice of the claim to victim status, society will resist pressure tactics, and such tactics will serve only to further alienation. No self-identified group of victims who are not the majority can achieve liberation by brute appeals to power and coercion. Herein lies the Achilles heel of most liberationist movements: they can all too easily use up their moral capital. When this happens, the majority grow tired and cynical of the victim's continued cry. Further, it is always possible to turn the liberationist strategy on the victim himself or herself. Even among liberals there is a growing, if only secretly uttered, resentment against those who claim to be society's victims' pointing the finger of guilt. People will not forever give assent to an indictment that ultimately calls into question one's right to exist. For example, well-off urban workers and dwellers who were initially sympathetic to the plight of the homeless have begun to resent their panhandling and squatting in public places. Polls now show a considerable shift in attitudes as the well-off conclude that the homeless are victimizing them. Such resentment easily degenerates into cynical one-upmanship as one interest group tries to out-victim the other. Because the impulse to liberation has become a cultural cliché—and further, as Reinhold Niebuhr never tired of reminding us, people always see the justice of their own interests more clearly then they see that of other people's—even righteous liberation rhetoric is in danger of being absorbed in a general, numbing ennui. In such a climate boredom and cynicism may finally prevail; it can only be countered if the true victims and their advocates maintain the high moral ground. This includes personal morality. Reinhold Niebuhr reminded us that moral persuasion without pressure is impotent. However, mere power in our present context—that is, power that plays or appeals to victimhood but dispenses with moral persuasion—will fail, for no group in our society has the power to gain its rights without widespread ethical consent, and such consent cannot be achieved if the victim does not inspire the idealism of the majority.

It is admittedly difficult for those who feel driven to resort to one form of pressure or coercion or another in order to push the victim's cause to the forefront, to make the shift from an assault upon oppression to the recognition that the oppressors must be won over. Vengeance may seem to be emotionally satisfying, but it is counterproductive, especially in a state where no minority can win true justice without bringing the majority to their point of view.

9. A few politicians still have a taste for witch-hunts, as Sen. Jesse Helms's recent assault upon the National Endowment for the Arts indicates. Nevertheless, Congress as a whole is presently disinclined to investigate "subversives" in academe or in the arts; we generally have been too indulged to be dangerous.

5

Theology, the Bible, and the Poor

James H. Cone

Sunday Morning, lithograph

Theology is language about God. Christian theology is language about God's liberating activity in the world on behalf of the poor and oppressed. Any talk about God that fails to make God's liberation of the poor its starting point is not Christian. It may be philosophical and have some relation to Scripture, but it is not Christian. For the word "Christian" connects theology inseparably to God's will to set the captives free.

   I realize that this understanding of theology and the gospel is not the central view of the Western theological tradition, and neither is it the dominant viewpoint of contemporary theology in Europe and North America. However, truth ought not to be defined by the intellectual interests of seminary and university academicians. My purpose here is to examine the *theological* presuppositions that underlie the claim that Christian theology is language about God's liberation of the poor from social and political oppression.

My contention that Christian theology is such language is based upon the assumption that Scripture is a primary source of Christian theological speech. That the Bible is important for Christian theology appears self-evident. Without this basic witness, Christianity would be meaningless. This point seems obvious to me, but it does need clarification. There are nearly as many perspectives on Scripture as there are theologians. Some regard it as infallible, and others say it is simply an important body of literature. While I cannot assess the validity of the major viewpoints, I can state what I believe to be the central message of Scripture.

The Bible is first and foremost a story of the Israelite people who believed that God was involved in their history. In the Old Testament, the story begins with the first Exodus of Hebrew slaves from Egypt and continues through the second Exodus from Babylon and the rebuilding of the temple. The import of the biblical message is clear on at least one point: God's salvation is revealed in the liberation of slaves from sociopolitical bondage. Indeed, God's judgment is inflicted on the people of Israel when they humiliate the poor and the orphans. "You shall not illtreat any widow or fatherless child. If you do, be sure that I will listen if they appeal to me; my anger will be roused and I will kill you with the sword" (Exod. 22:23–24, NEB). Other themes in the Old Testament are important, but their importance lies in their illumination of the central theme of God's liberation of the poor. To fail to see this is to misunderstand and distort the message of the Old Testament.

My contention that Scripture is the story of God's liberation of the poor also applies to the New Testament, where the story is carried to universal dimensions. The meaning of Jesus Christ is found in God's will to make liberation not simply the property of one people, but of all humankind. God became a poor Jew in Jesus and thus identified with the helpless in Israel. The cross of Jesus is nothing but God's will to be with and like the poor. The resurrection means that God achieved victory over oppression, so that the poor no longer have to be determined by their poverty. This is true not only for the house of Israel, but of all the wretched of the land. The Incarnation, then, is simply God's taking upon the divine self human suffering and humiliation. The resurrection is the divine victory over suffering, the bestowal of freedom on all who are weak and helpless. This is the central meaning of the biblical story.

If theology is derived from this divine story, it must be a language about liberation. Anything else would be an ideological distortion of the gospel message.

Because theology begins with Scripture, it must also begin with Jesus Christ. Christian theology is language about the crucified and risen Christ who grants freedom to all who are wrongly condemned in an oppressive society. Christ is the poor person's victory over poverty. If theology does not take this seriously, how can it be worthy of the name Christian? If the church, the community out of which theology arises, does not make God's liberation of the poor central in its mission and proclamation, how can it rest easy with a poor Jew as the dominant symbol of its message?

Because Christian theology is more than the retelling of the biblical story, it also must do more than interpret Scripture. The message of Scripture is not always self-evident; therefore, it is theology's task to interpret it in the human situation. And because theological ideas do not fall from heaven but are made by people seeking meaning in the world, theology must use other sources in addition to Scripture. To deny that our language about God is inseparably bound with our own historicity is to become enslaved to our own ideology.

The issue, then, is not whether we can or ought to avoid speaking of human culture in the doing of theology. The question is whether the Scripture bears witness to something about God that is not simply about ourselves. Unless this possibility is given, however limited it might be, there seems to be no point in talking about the distinction between white theology and Black theology or the difference between falsehood and truth.

By focusing on Scripture, theology is granted the freedom to take seriously its social and political situation without being exclusively determined by it. Thus, the question is how and in what way we take it seriously. Whose social situation does our theology represent? For whom do we speak? The importance of Scripture in our theology is that it can help us answer that question so as to represent the political interest of the One about whom Christianity speaks. By using Scripture, we are forced by it to focus on our social existence, but not merely in terms of our own interests. Scripture can liberate theology to be Christian in the contemporary situation. It can free the theologians and preachers from their social ideologies and enable them to hear a word that is other than their own consciousness.

This "other" in theology is distinct but never separated from our social existence. God became human in Christ so that we are free to speak about God in terms of humanity. Indeed, any other talk is not about the crucified and risen Lord. The presence of the crucified and risen Christ as witnessed in Scripture determines whose social interest we must represent if we are to be faithful to him.

In an attempt to do theology in the light of this biblical witness to the crucified and risen Christ as he is found in our contemporary situation, I have spoken of Christian theology as Black theology. Of course there are other ways of talking about God that are also Christian. Christian theology can be written from an Indian perspective and an African viewpoint. It can be written in the light of women's experience; thus, we hear about feminist and womanist theologies. In Japan, I have been impressed by the way that Korean Christians are hearing the word of divine liberation in an oppressive Japanese culture. In Korea, Koreans speak about Minjung theology, which translated means "a theology of the poor." Christian theology can also be written from the perspective of class, as has been clearly and profoundly disclosed in the writings of Latin American liberation theologians. It is also possible to combine the issues of class, sex, and color, as many Asians, Africans, Latin Americans, and U.S. minority theologians are currently doing in the Ecumenical Association of Third World Theologians (EATWOT). There is not one Christian theology, but many Christian theologies that are valid expressions of the gospel of Jesus.

But it is not possible to do Christian theology apart from the biblical claim that God came in Christ to set the captives free. Indeed, there can be no Christian speech about God which does not represent the interest of the poor, the victims in society. If we can make that point an embodiment of our Christian identity and our Christian preaching, we will have moved a long way since the days of Constantine.

Because Christian theology is language about God's liberation of the weak as defined by Scripture in the context of our contemporary struggle for justice, it is inseparably connected with an oppressed community. How can we speak correctly about God unless our language arises out of the community where God's presence is found? If Christian theology is language about the crucified and risen One, the One who has elected all for freedom, what else can it be other than the language of those who are fighting for freedom?

My limitation of Christian theology to the oppressed community does not mean that everything the oppressed say about God is correct simply because they are weak and helpless. To do so would be to equate their word with God's word. Nothing in Scripture grants this possibility. When the oppressed use their position as a privilege, as an immunity from error, they would do well to remember the biblical witness to God's righteousness against all who claim to be God.

When I limit Christian theology to the oppressed community, I intend to say nothing other than what I believe to be the central message of Scripture: God has chosen to disclose divine righteousness in the liberation of the poor. Therefore, to be outside of this community is to be in a place where one is excluded from the possibility of hearing and obeying God's word of liberation. By becoming poor and entrusting divine revelation to a carpenter from Nazareth, God made clear where one has to be in order to hear the divine Word and experience divine presence. If Jesus had been born in the king's court and had been an advisor to the emperor of Rome, what I am saying would have no validity. If Jesus had made no distinction between the rich and the poor, the weak and the strong, the Christian message would not be one of liberation for the oppressed. If Jesus had not been condemned as a blasphemer by the religious leaders of his time and crucified as a criminal of Rome, my claim about Christian theology and the oppressed would be meaningless. It is because Scripture is so decisively clear on this issue that I insist that Christian theology cannot separate itself from the cultural history of the oppressed if it intends to be faithful to the One who makes Christian language possible.

What then are we to say about these other so-called Christian theologies? To the extent that they fail to remain faithful to the central message of the gospel, they are heretical. In saying this, I do not intend to suggest that I have the whole truth. In fact, I could be the heretic. The purpose of identifying heresy is not to be able to distinguish "good" people from "bad" or infallible truth from error. I merely intend to say what I believe to be faithful to the gospel of Jesus as witnessed in Scripture and as revealed in the struggles of the poor for freedom. If we do not say what we believe, in love and faith and hope, then why speak at all? If there is no distinction between truth and error, the gospel and heresy, then there is no way to say what Christian theology is. We must be able to say when language is not Christian. The identification of heresy is not because I want to burn anybody at the stake. Far too many of my people have been lynched for me to suggest such nonsense. To know what heresy is, is to know what appears to be truth but is actually untruth. Thus, it is for the sake of the truth of the gospel that we must say what truth is not.

The saying of what truth is, is intimately connected with the doing of truth. To know the truth is to do the truth. What we say can be authenticated only by what we do. Unfortunately, the Western church has not always been clear on this point. Its mistake often has been the identification of heresy with word rather than action, confession rather than action. It has been more concerned with orthodoxy rather than orthopraxis. By failing to explicate the connection between word and action, the church tended to identify the gospel with "right" speech and thus became the chief heretic. It became so preoccupied with its own spoken word about God that it failed to hear and thus live according to God's word of freedom for the poor. From Augustine to Barth, it is hard to find a theologian in the Western church who defines the gospel in terms of God's liberation of the oppressed.

The same is true in much of the contemporary speech about God. It can be seen in the separation of theology from ethics and the absence of liberation in both. The chief mistake of contemporary white theology is not found simply in what it says about God. It is found in its separation of theory from praxis, and the absence of liberation in its analysis of the gospel.

The limitation of Christian theology to the oppressed community not only helps us identify heresy, it also helps us reexamine the sources of theological speech. The language of liberation must reflect the experiences of the people about whom we claim to speak. To say that one's speech is a theology of liberation does not in itself mean that it represents the oppressed. There are many theologies of liberation, not all of which represent the weak and the helpless. The difference between liberation theology in general and liberation theology from the Christian perspective is whether the language about freedom is derived from one's solidarity with the oppressed people's struggle for freedom. If so, it is Christian language. It is a language that is accountable to the God encountered in the oppressed community, not some abstract God in a theological textbook. To say that one's theology represents the poor means that the representation reflects the words and deeds of the poor. The theologian begins to talk like the poor, to pray like the poor, and to preach with the poor in mind. Instead of making Barth, Tillich, and Pannenberg the primary sources for the doing of theology, a true liberation theologian is compelled to hear the cries of the people who sing: "I wish I knew how it would feel to be free, I wish I could break all the chains holdin' me."

What would theology look like if we were to take seriously the claim that Christian speech is poor people's speech about their hopes and dreams that one day "trouble will be no more"? One thing is certain: it would not look like most of the papers presented in theological and philosophical societies in Europe and America, and in learned meetings in the Third World that imitate them.

Theology derived from the moans and shouts of oppressed Black people defines a different set of problems than those found in the white theological textbooks. Instead of asking whether the Bible is infallible, Black people want to know whether it is real—that is, whether the God to which it bears witness is present in their struggle. Black theology seeks to investigate the meaning of Black people's confidence in the biblical claim that Jesus is the way, the truth, and the life. Black theology is the consciousness of the oppressed Blacks analyzing the meaning of their faith when they have to live in extreme suffering. How can Black theology remain faithful to the people and the God revealed in their struggle if it does not take seriously the people's conceptualizations of their claim that "God will make a way of no way"? They really believe that

When you are troubled, burdened with care,
And know not what to do;
Fear ye not to call His Name
And He will fix it for you.

Theology derived from the Black experience must reflect the rhythm and the mood, the passion and the ecstasy, the joy and the sorrow of a people in a struggle to free themselves from the shackles of oppression. This theology must be Black because the people are Black. It must deal with liberation because the people are oppressed. It must be biblical because the people believe that the God of the Exodus and the prophets and of Jesus and the apostle Paul is involved in their history, liberating them from bondage. A theology derived from Black sources would have to focus on Jesus Christ as the beginning and the end of faith, because this affirmation is a summary of the Black testimony that "Jesus picked me up, turned me round, left my feet on solid ground." He is sometimes called the "Wheel in the middle of the Wheel," the "Rose of Sharon," and the "Lord of Life." Black people believe that he healed the sick, gave sight to the blind, and enabled the lame to walk. "Jesus," they say, "do most anything."

The presence of Jesus as the starting point of Black theology does not mean that the theology can overlook the continued presence of suffering in Black life. How can we claim that "God will fix it" for the poor when the poor still live in poverty? The blues, folklore, and other secular expressions are constant reminders that a simplistic view of divine liberation is never adequate for a people in struggle against oppression. And Black religion has never been silent on the theme of suffering. Indeed, Black faith arose out of Black people's experience of suffering. Without the brokenness of Black existence, its pain and sorrow, there would be no reason for the existence of Black faith.

Nobody knows the trouble I've seen,
Nobody knows my sorrow,
Nobody knows the trouble I've seen,
Glory, Hallelujah!

The "Glory Hallelujah" at the end of that spiritual is not a denial of trouble but an affirmation of faith that trouble does not have the last word on Black existence. It means that evil and suffering, while unquestionably present, cannot count decisively against Black people's faith that Jesus is also present with them, fighting against trouble. His divine presence counts more than the pain that the people experience and have experienced in their history. Jesus is the people's "rock in a weary land" and their "shelter in a time of storm." No matter how difficult the pains of life might become, they cannot destroy the people's confidence that victory over suffering has already been won in Jesus' resurrection. Thus, the people sing:

Sometimes I hangs my head an' cries,
But Jesus going to wipe my weep'n eyes.

Of course, there is no evidence that Black people's faith claim is objectively or scientifically true. Thus, when critics of Black theology ask about the decisive liberation event in Black history, they are asking the question from a vantage point that is external to Black faith. Black faith claims that Jesus is the only evidence one needs to be assured that God has not left the little ones alone in bondage. For those who stand outside of this faith, such a claim is a scandal—it is foolishness to those whose wisdom is derived from European intellectual history. "But to those who are called, . . . Christ [is] the power of God, and the wisdom of God" (1 Cor. 1:24). In Black religion, Christ is the Alpha and Omega, the One who has come to make the first last and the last first. The knowledge of this truth is not found in philosophy, sociology, or psychology. It is found in the immediate presence of Jesus with the people, "buildin' them up where they are torn down and proppin' them up on every leanin' side." The evidence that Jesus is liberating them from bondage is found in their walking and talking with him, telling him about their troubles. It is found in the courage and strength he bestows on the people as they struggle to humanize their environment.

These answers will not satisfy the problem of theodicy as defined by Western philosophy. But Black faith assertions were never intended to be answers for the intellectual problems that arise from the European experience. They are Black reflections on life and are intended as testimonies so that the oppressed would not give up in despair. They are not rational arguments. The truth of the claims is not found in whether the Black faith perspective answers the theodicy problem as posed by Camus's *The Plague* or Sartre's *Being and Nothingness*. The truth of the Black faith claim is found in whether the people receive the extra strength to fight until freedom comes. Its truth is found in whether the people who are the victims of Western philosophy and theology are led to struggle to realize the freedom that they talk about.

The same is true for a Black theology or philosophy that seeks to speak on behalf of the people. Pure theory is for those who have the leisure for reflection, not for the victims of the land. The truth, therefore, of any theological analysis ought to be decided by the practical function of our assertions in the community we claim to represent. What does your theology cause people to do? That is the essential question that every theologian should be prepared to answer. An analysis of Black faith, with Jesus as the "Captain of the Old Ship of Zion," can lead the people to believe that their fight is not in vain. That was why Martin Luther King, Jr., could move Black people to fight for justice. He had a dream that was connected with Jesus. Without Jesus, the people would have remained passive and content with humiliation and suffering.

When I evaluate Western philosophy's analysis of metaphysics and ontology, I do not know whether King was right, if rightness is defined by an abstract rationality unrelated to the people's struggle. But in the faith context of Black religion, King was right, because the people were led to act out the faith they talked about. If Black theology is to be a theology of and for this Black faith, it will not try to reconcile the logic of its assertions with Western theology and philosophy. On the contrary, Black theologians should develop a theological methodology that supports Black people who sing:

Without God I could no nothing;
Without God my life would fail;
Without God my life would be rugged,
Just like a ship without a sail.

Note the absence of philosophical skepticism in the next verse.

Without a doubt, God is my Savior,
Yes, my strength along the way;
Yes, in deep water, God is my anchor,
And through faith God will keep me all the way.

It is because Black people feel secure in "leaning and depending on Jesus" that they often lift their voices in praise and adoration, singing:

"Thank you Jesus, I thank you Lord. For you brought me a mighty long ways. You've been my doctor, you've been my lawyer, and you've been my friend. You've been my everything!" These people believe that with Jesus' presence, they cannot lose. Victory over suffering and oppression is certain, if not now, then in God's own "good time." "One day, it will all be over." We will "cross the river of Jordan" and "sit down with the Father and argue with the Son" and "tell them about the world we just come from." Thus, Black people's struggle for freedom is not in vain. This is what Blacks mean when they sing: "I'm so glad that trouble don't last always." Because trouble does not have the last word, we can fight in order to realize in our present what we know to be coming in God's future.

NOTE

For a further discussion of the theme of suffering in Black religion, see "God and Black Suffering" in my book *The Spirituals and the Blues* (New York: Seabury Press, 1972) and chapter 8, "Divine Liberation and Black Suffering," in *God of the Oppressed* (New York: Seabury Press, 1975). This theme has been much discussed by other Black writers; see especially William Jones, *Is God a White Racist?* (New York: Doubleday, 1973).

III

Homiletics

No School Today, lithograph

6

Preaching, Hermeneutics, and Liberation

David G. Buttrick

For more than two hundred years, preaching has been tied to a historical-critical method of biblical exegesis. This approach to Scripture arose as a pseudoscientific method promising some degree of scholarly objectivity free from dogmatic concerns. Following the thought of Descartes, the method combined radical skepticism with judgments of objective reason. Certainly, historical-critical exegesis has been productive. In libraries we can wander past Kittel's multivolume "Wordbooks" as well as shelves of commentaries, from the early *International Critical Commentary* to recent volumes of *Hermeneia,* and be in awe of erudition.

But in the late 1950s questions began to multiply. Rudolf Bultmann asked if "objective" presuppositionless exegesis is actually possible; do not exegetes come to texts with inevitable pre-understandings?[1] More recently the Critical Theory of the so-called Frankfurt School with more than a dash of Marxist suspicion has raised questions with regard to the political, social, and economic commitments of "establishment" critics.[2] Feminist theorists and liberation theologians have added still more fuel to the hermeneutic fire.[3] How can middle-class, predominantly white, generally masculine mainline clergy read biblical texts with any kind of innocence? Though Paul Ricoeur may propose a second naiveté following after a hermeneutics of suspicion, is such a naiveté even conceivable?[4]

Let us look at some areas in which we may have been blinded by the mind-set of mainline American Christianity.

THE RISE OF THE PERSONALIST PULPIT

There seems little doubt that the Christian Scriptures regard sin as a kind of collective captivity; we are gripped by sin under the domination of "principalities and powers." Though Paul may wrestle with an inward dimension of sin in the seventh chapter of Romans, elsewhere he depicts sin as a kind of social bondage.[5] We are captives to the mind of "this present age" and incapable of achieving our own liberation. Of course, if the Scriptures depict sin as social captivity, they also look for social salvation. Did not Jesus announce an imminent Kingdom of God, God's new order, and call people into a new humanity?—"The time is fulfilled, the Kingdom of God is at hand; repent and believe in the Gospel."[6] Paul seems to have much the same understanding; he believes the new aeon of God is imminent, and regards the community of faith as an advance guard of the new aeon and a locus of liberation.[7]

Nevertheless, following the cue proffered by Harry Emerson Fosdick's Project Method and his early interest in the "new psychology," coupled with the existentialist mind of the fifties, the American pulpit imaged sin and salvation largely in personalist, inward terms.[8] Sin was understood to be an inward problem (hubris) showing itself in fear, guilt, hostility, and anxiety.[9] In turn, salvation was an inner reconciliation, a psychological newness, characterized by love, peace, and above all, self-acceptance. The turn to such a scheme was easy enough; had not America been taught "heart religion" by the sweep of nineteenth-century pietistic revivalism? The result has been nicely documented by Robert Bellah and a team of social analysts in *Habits of the Heart*.[10] From the East Coast, where "positive thinking" has been in vogue, to the West, where "possibility thinking" has built a glass cathedral, most mainline pulpits have plunged headlong into what Philip Rieff labeled "the triumph of the therapeutic."[11]

The result has been a twofold disaster. First, the nature of God has been determined by our psychological problems. God has become a care-giver who accepts us therapeutically reducing our inner conflict and increasing our self-esteem. God's divine agenda appears to be our psychological well-being. Second, the prophetic, ethical tradition has all but disappeared from mainline pulpits. For this tradition to flourish, sin must have social dimension and salvation must be corporate. At a time when American power is questionable, mainline Protestant pulpits, for the most part preaching to Reagan/Bush devotees, have been tragically silent. Heart religion has swept the day.

The real problem has been a personalist hermeneutics. Preachers read biblical texts as if they were addressed to a single, psychologically beset person. Ethical passages are addressed to individual Christians in their own decision making, in spite of all the corporate "you"s in the Greek text. Theological pericopes having to do with sin and salvation are read as if they pertained to a prototypical self-in-existence. But the Hebrew and Christian Scriptures are rather obviously written to and for *communities*—indeed, communities with communal consciousness. To reduce such texts to a personalist, existentialist model is to engage in a hermeneutic lobotomy in which social consciousness is lopped off and discarded before preachers enter their pulpits.

THE LOSS OF SOCIAL LIBERATION

Years ago, Reinhold Niebuhr's colleague, John Bennett, argued that communism was a kind of Christian heresy.[12] His remarks were suggestive. Clearly, early Christianity was primarily a slave religion; it spread among the poor, it promised liberation, and according to the book of Acts, it produced a form of communism with respect to property.[13] Though Ananias and Sapphira were early exponents of free enterprise, the Holy Spirit seemed to be backing a policy of shared wealth.[14] Underlying the social policies of early Christianity was an eager anticipation of the Kingdom of God that, according to our Lord, was at hand. Thus, the primitive Christian enterprise was animated by social vision and by the looming image of God's new order in which the poor would inevitably inherit the earth. Whether such early idealism must be moderated by "Christian realism," as Reinhold Niebuhr insisted, is a moot question.[15] The fact is that texts speaking of wealth and poverty cannot be grasped apart from the so-called communism of the early Christian community. The texts are not personal financial planning advice for individual Christians; instead, they call us into a new-order Christian community of sharing.

How has the American pulpit handled texts having to do with wealth and poverty, texts which presuppose common property in contrast to private ownership? Not well. In mainline churches, we preach to a middle-class Protestant people who, having achieved a modicum of fiscal security, are easily threatened by anything that even hints at communal claim on their property. Moreover, our churches seem to be operating in a free-enterprise system of competitive denominationalism catering to consumer souls in a religious marketplace. Therefore, whenever we stumble on a text having to do with cash, we preach with a degree of queasiness, putting forth a morality of moderation—in essence, "Don't be *too* greedy."

The problem lies deeper still. In Jesus' preaching, as well as in early Christian sermons, the Kingdom of God was a social image that depicted a new sociopolitical order under the rule of God. In our preaching, we have tempered the image. Either we have retained the idea of the Reign as a kind of manana theology, a utopian idealism that need not be expected to shape reality in the near future, or we have regarded the Reign as a realm of faith—believers, by believing, enter it in much the same way that children, by imagining, enter fairy-tale realms. In either case, the sharp social criticism implicit in the idea of the Reign is mitigated, and the real social demands of life in the Reign are banished to into a never-never land of religious fancy.

We could write off such strategies as nothing more than typical theological misinterpretation if it were not for the fact that they seem to avoid collision with prevalent capitalist ideology. They are palatable to our middle-class congregations and competitively wise in a denominational free market. If primitive Christianity were preached, it might sound like theological liberalism, and who, in the land of the Bush and the Quayle, wants to be a liberal *anything* these days? As a result, the communal vision of the Christian Scriptures remains largely unpreached. When we are trying to make it in the present social order, who needs the gospel of a *new* social order?

WHITE, MALE, MIDDLE-CLASS, AND PROTESTANT

In Protestant communities, the ministry is predominantly white, male, and middle class. (In Catholic communities, the priesthood follows much the same pattern.) In a land where established power is likewise ordered by those who are male Caucasians of Anglo-European descent, a tacit alliance of "likes" has formed a studied insensitivity to minority affairs. We speak to our own kind. We think as our own kind. Thus, it is difficult for us to read texts addressed to oppressed Israel, a people who emerged from slavery in Egypt, or to early Christian communities that were primarily composed of the poor. We simply do not think that way! Whether innocently or by subtle intent, we read texts as if they were addressed to a white, male, middle-class establishment, oblivious to the hermeneutics of African-Americans or of women.

We must not tumble into a logic that denies Scripture to the socially dominant. We cannot argue that the Bible can only be understood by the poor or the oppressed. Too many texts in the Christian Scriptures presuppose an economically mixed community. And certainly prophetic denunciations of careless affluence were not written merely to inflame the underclass. Luther's dictum, "We are beggars all," may suggest an appropriate posture for the reading of Scripture. Nevertheless, America is a relatively well-fed nation in a hungry world, and in America white, male Protestants have been decidedly privileged. Middle-class mainline Protestantism simply cannot conceive God's special preference for the oppressed, particularly the economically oppressed. Bias is inevitable.

The situation today is in flux. Social analysts suggest that the white Protestant population in America is dwindling and that by the year 2050 our country will be composed predominantly of Spanish-speaking, African-American, and Asian-American peoples.[16] Once-dominant mainline white Protestant congregations are in decline. The so-called Protestant era is over. In such a time of transition we hear many new and worthwhile voices. Feminist theology *is* important. African-American theology *is* important. Spanish-speaking liberationist theology *is* important. Though such voices may threaten the identity of a predominantly white, male clerical establishment, the church must listen carefully, for theological understanding is ultimately at stake. Certainly we can no longer embrace a Barthian biblical positivism in the midst of vocal pluralism. In fact, Barthian biblical positivism itself may well be *the* bias of a white European Protestant clergy. Certainly the Barthian position is not altogether hospitable to the clamor of cultural minorities![17]

GOOD NEWS FOR THE POOR

We have suggested that the Bible is a book for minority people who are well aware of their status. Israelites were a minority in the ancient world; they lived in a bathmat-sized land surrounded by powers. The powers changed—Assyria, Babylon, Egypt, Persia, Rome—but always they were crushing powers, compared to struggling Israel. When we flip to Christian Scriptures, the situation is scarcely improved. How does Paul describe his Corinthian congregation? Not many rich, not many wise, not many with social status![18] Christian congregations were evidently at the bottom of the social ladder and, for the most part, must have remained so for decades, perhaps until the time of the Constantinian approval. They may well have seen their social status as "deprived" and, therefore, dreamed of God's promised Reign in which, according to the Lord, social status might be tipped topsy-turvy.

The message of God's new order, while unnerving to the socially dominant and invested, is greeted with enthusiasm by the outcast. Though Marx regarded Christian eschatology as a delusion designed to dissuade the proletariat from seizing social power, he was attacking a vertical, spatial, pie-in-the-sky eschatology.[19] Early Christian eschatology, emerging from the social vision of the Hebrew tradition, prophetic and apocalyptic, was defined temporally and thus horizontally.[20] Early Christian communities looked for a Kingdom of God; their vision was social and eschatological. Moreover, their evangelism was not so much a "come to Jesus and get saved" message as an invitation to join a new humanity inaugurated in Jesus Christ. They saw themselves as a proleptic sign of God's new order, although living in the broken humanity of "this present age." In the new order, there would be neither Jew nor Greek, neither slave nor free, neither male nor female—and indeed, neither rich nor poor.[21]

It is precisely the poverty of early Christianity that calls into question the hermeneutics of a status clergy. Is oppression, or at very least solidarity with the oppressed, a prerequisite for biblical understanding? How can a Constantinian church recover and embrace the radical eschatology of the early Christian gospel?

Fosdick's therapeutic emphasis and Barth's dialectical biblicism had little impact on African-American preaching. White Protestant pulpits were clearly captivated: either they dove headlong into the therapeutic, preaching a personalist gospel to psychologically self-aware people, or they leapt onto the Barthian bandwagon and preached the Bible to the faithful of the church, diffidently ignoring both cultural mind and cultural movements. But, though learned Black preachers

read both Barth and Fosdick, African-American sermons did not succumb to either movement. The interesting question is, Why not?[22]

THE POWER OF THE BLACK PULPIT

Except recently in "Buppie" churches, therapeutic preaching
has made little headway among African-American congregations. We
can point to two probable reasons. First, Black congregations have a
stronger common consciousness than do most white Protestant congregations. This Black consciousness offers a sense of common identity
and, perhaps, common psychology. Therefore, African-American congregations can be said to have a common mind in a way that individualistic white congregations do not. Second, Black consciousness includes
a common awareness of the demeaning nature of racism that over-
whelms individual psychologies. Therefore, personal therapeutic projects are not the crucial concern of the gospel; liberation is. A sense of
common predicament redefines every personal quandary. We simply
cannot imagine Fosdick's personalist agendas captivating African-
American congregations. So, though Black preachers have learned from
Fosdick's rhetorical techniques, they appear to have avoided his psychological personalism.

Barth's influence is more difficult to analyze. Certainly his dialectical method, which set biblical revelation over against all cultural wis-
doms, would win enthusiastic approval in Black communities. After
all, African-American preaching has again and again set the biblical
promises of God against the sinful racism of society. Just as Barth was
embraced by the social protesters of the sixties, so his sharp dialectic,
his suspicion of established culture "religion," and his stress on the tri-
umphant Word of God would be welcomed by many if not all Black
clergy. After all, one of the ever-present features of the Black sermon is
a kind of laughter over the foolish pretensions of an obtuse society that
cannot grasp God's liberating purposes. Nevertheless, though predis-
posed to Barthian theology, the African-American community did not
succumb to Barth's biblical positivism. Why not?

The Bible plays a sophisticated role in the Black preaching tradition.[23] In African-American pulpits it is read more as a story than as history. That is, issues of historicity are not primary, and historical-critical
research is rarely the method of choice. We do not suggest that Black

preachers treat Scripture as fiction; they do not. But among African-Americans the common memory of the community is shaped by story-telling, and therefore, biblical materials, particularly the narrative texts of the Hebrew Scriptures, are read as hand-me-down community sto-ries, the stories of God and God's people. What's more, biblical stories are preached as perennial tales that are still contemporary to God's people. The narrative structure of the Black sermon prevents the histor-ical objectivity that distances Scripture in most white Protestant pul-pits. The same narrative/immediate approach to biblical material has saved the Black pulpit from the stridencies of the American fundamen-talist movement.

Also, in African-American pulpits the Bible is read more as an es-chatological promise than as a past event. Biblical material is not so much past-tense revelation as it is a present-tense witness to what God is bringing about today and, above all, where God is leading us in the promised future. Scripture is interpreted in the light of the promises of God. Black eschatology, contrary to Marc Connelly's caricature of Black folk religion in *The Green Pastures*, is not merely focused on heavenly spaces;[24] in many ways it is still horizontal and informed by the social vi-sion of the prophetic tradition. Thus, it is closer to the two-aeon think-ing of the Christian Scriptures than is often realized. God's final pur-pose is a redeemed society free from deprivation, racism, oppression, and social dominations. Clearly, Black preaching envisions Shalom. More, Black preaching celebrates in anticipation of God's sure prom-ises.

We have reviewed some of the African-American tradition not as an expiation of liberal white guilt, but to suggest some features of a lib-eration hermeneutics that may help mainline preaching extricate itself from the therapeutic "self-enrichment" and biblical positivism, both of which have led to a loss of prophetic edge in the pulpit. We have con-cluded: (1) Scripture must not be interpreted as addressing an existen-tial self in self-awareness but as speaking to a common Christian con-sciousness; (2) Scripture must be interpreted in solidarity with victims;[25] (3) Scripture must be read as stories of God that also happen to be *our* stories; and (4) Scripture must be read in the light of God's social prom-ises, i.e., a new order. Such a hermeneutics may save us from the per-sonalism, historicism, and biblical positivism that have silenced the prophetic word of God.

TOWARD HERMENEUTIC REVISION

To expand upon the above conclusions:

Scripture must not be interpreted as addressing an existential self in self-awareness but as speaking to a common Christian consciousness. The injunction sounds as if we are buying into a Barthian model in which the objective Word of God in Scripture addresses the faith of the church. Cannot Scripture speak to the unchurched secularist? Does not the Word of God speak to human being *as* human being? Two comments may be in order. First, evangelism may not speak from biblical texts at all. A right evangelism is not based on busing people into buildings where Bibles are; properly, evangelism speaks in secular places in a secular style, though it may be theologically acute and/or biblically based. Second, "common Christian consciousness" is always an admixture.[26] Though we are not of the world, we are in the world. Thus, common Christian consciousness is peculiarly twofold—worldly *un*wise and at the same time shaped by symbols of revelation. Our initial claim rejects an existential personalism that leaves little room for social meaning.[27]

Scripture must be interpreted in solidarity with victims. This statement appropriately follows the previous one. Personalist preaching, in offering models of personal salvation, actually fosters a neglect of others, particularly of socially disadvantaged others. Of course, exclusivist notions of salvation, personal or social, could result in the same disdain and social neglect; in effect, we are saved and, ha ha, you are not. Christian faith, though particularly Christian, rightly envisions a new order that is eschatologically larger than its own community; though a determinate community, its hope is indeterminate in character.[28] In other words, the Christian community is one with the wide humanity God calls and, indeed, regards the wide humanity as family before God. The real question posed by liberationists is, Can a middle-class church comprehend the minds of those who are economically or racially oppressed? To accept such a conclusion is to adopt a cynicism the Bible refuses. A middle-class American mentality is obviously not congenial to a hermeneutics of deprivation. But we have argued that Christian consciousness is inevitably double-minded; Christian imagination can share a wider, more humane consciousness. In fact, Christian consciousness by definition may always be in solidarity with victims—after all, our Lord was hauled before power people, was tossed in a Jerusalem drunk tank, was made a victim of police brutality, and was obscenely crucified.

Scripture must be read as stories of God that also happen to be our *stories.* We accept this dictum as a corrective to historicist readings of Scripture that, in an age of "revelation-in-history," may be "riveting every daybreak to the past." But there is a danger: if we read the Scriptures as *our* stories, that is, as leading to our communal existence, narrative theology can lead to an exclusive community quite detached from what Pannenberg labels "universal history."[29] Anamnesis can be perverse. On the other hand, to live *in* a story of God that is moving toward some eschatological denouement that is larger than the Christian community—toward Zion, indeed toward a universal Shalom—is a good basis for liberation hope. Those homileticians who too easily embrace the category of "story" must be wary; narrative is only one of many biblical languages. Moreover, story per se can be demonic, actually obliterating theological depth. Nevertheless, story can address faith, setting it free from the past and from the literalism of the historicist grasp of Scripture. Story can also illuminate the recurring patterns of our common life before God.

Scripture must be read in the light of God's social promises, i.e., a new order. Feminists have noted that a biblical positivism can lead readers into the chill embrace of a "Total Woman"; the Bible may well reflect a paternal social order. As a result, some feminists have argued for a reading of Scripture in the light of its eschatological vision.[30] Certainly, African-American communities have cherished eschatological promises, and Spanish liberation theologies are based on social vision. While eschatology has offered pie-in-the-sky to oppressed social classes as a reason to put up and shut up with regard to systemic deprivation, it has also offered images of new order that have been revolutionary in their impact.[31] So, although we must never forget Nietzsche's critique of eschatology, we must also learn to sing the social vision of the spirituals.[32] In the eschatological notion of God's new order are images of an indeterminate future that can correct the blindness of our determinate perspectives. The Bible must be read in the light of the future of God that it portends.

If we are to preach "good news to the poor" (Luke 4:18) in middle-class churches, the crucial problem is hermeneutics. How can we read Scripture as liberation? How can sermons be set free from the limitations of therapy on the one hand and a Barthian biblical positivism on the other? We have indicated a few concerns. The gospel is for the poor and for those who are willing to become poor for its sake. We need eyes to see and, yes, ears to hear.

NOTES

1. See Rudolf Bultmann, *Jesus Christ and Mythology* (New York: Charles Scribner's Sons, 1958), chapters 1–3, and also the discussion in R. Bultmann et al., *Kerygma and Myth: A Theological Debate* (New York: Harper & Brothers, 1961).

2. On Critical Theory, see David Held, *Introduction to Critical Theory: Horkheimer to Habermas* (Berkeley: University of California Press, 1980), and Raymond Geuss, *The Idea of a Critical Theory: Habermas and the Frankfort School* (Cambridge: Cambridge University Press, 1981).

3. On feminist hermeneutics, see Elisabeth Schüssler Fiorenza, *Bread Not Stone: The Challenge of Feminist Biblical Interpretation* (Boston: Beacon Press, 1984), and Letty M. Russell, ed., *Feminist Interpretation of the Bible* (Philadelphia: Westminster, 1985). On liberation hermeneutics, see J. S. Croatt, "Biblical Hermeneutics in the Theologies of Liberation," in *Irruption of the Third World: Challenge to Theology,* ed. V. Fabella and S. Torres (Maryknoll, NY: Orbis Books, 1983), 140–68.

4. See Paul Ricoeur, *The Symbolism of Evil* (Boston: Beacon Press, 1967), 347–57.

5. The notion of sin as bondage has been underscored by many Pauline interpreters; for example, see Victor P. Furnish, *Theology and Ethics in Paul* (Nashville: Abingdon Press, 1968), 135–42; J. Christiaan Beker, *Paul the Apostle* (Philadelphia: Fortress Press, 1980), chapter 10; and the discussion in Daniel Patte, *Paul's Faith and the Power of the Gospel* (Philadelphia: Fortress Press, 1983), 251–77.

6. See my argument in *Preaching Jesus Christ* (Philadelphia: Fortress Press, 1988), chapter 4.

7. See Beker, *Paul the Apostle,* chapter 10.

8. See my analysis, "Preaching in an *Un*brave New World," *Spire* 13, no. 1 (Summer/Fall 1988).

9. Though Niebuhr saw the profound connection between sin and anxiety, the therapeutic pulpit is seldom as sophisticated.

10. Robert N. Bellah et al., *Habits of the Heart: Individualism and Commitment in American Life* (San Francisco: Harper & Row, 1985).

11. Phillip Rieff, *The Triumph of the Therapeutic* (New York: Harper & Row, 1966; Chicago: University of Chicago Press, 1987).

12. John C. Bennett, *Christianity and Communism* (New York: Association Press, 1949), chapter 3.

13. It is notoriously difficult to detail what Acts means by "they had all things in common." See discussions in F. J. Foakes Jackson and Kirsopp Lake, in *The Beginnings of Christianity. Part I: The Acts of the Apostles*, vol. 5, ed. Krisopp Lake and Henry J. Cadbury (London: Macmillan, 1933), 140–51; J. Dupont, "Community of Goods in the Early Church," in *The Salvation of the Gentiles: Essays on the Acts of the Apostles* (New York: Paulist Press, 1979), 85–102; and most recently, Luke T. Johnson, *Sharing Possessions* (Philadelphia: Fortress Press, 1981). For a provocative if somewhat overstated interpretation, see José Miranda, *Communism in the Bible* trans. R. R. Barr (Maryknoll, NY: Orbis Books, 1982).

14. Acts 5:1–11.

15. See Reinhold Niebuhr, "When Will Christians Stop Fooling Themselves?" in *Love and Justice,* ed. D. B. Robertson (Cleveland: World Publishing, 1967), 40–46.

16. See "Beyond the Melting Pot," *Time* 135, no. 15 (9 April 1990): 28–31.

17. Barth's antithesis of biblical revelation and culture could well protect social domination in an unsavory way. In 1932 and 1933, Barth conducted a seminar on preaching, in the course of which he commented on the dangers of relevance: "Application . . . does not always have to be *à jour*. We do not always have to bring in the latest and most sensational events. For instance, if a fire broke out in the community last week, and church members are still suffering under its awful impact, we should be on guard against even hinting at this theme in the sermon. It belongs to everyday life, but now it is Sunday." Barth confessed with regret having mentioned World War I in his own sermons. "Pastors," he wrote, "should aim their guns beyond the hills of relevance." *Homiletics: The Nature and Preparation of the Sermon,* trans. Geoffrey W. Bromily with Donald E. Daniels (Unpublished manuscript). In South Africa, Allan Boesak might not agree.

18. 1 Cor. 1:26.

19. Bertolt Brecht, an aesthetic Marxist, sings a parody hymn celebrating Christian hope:

> And the grass, oh, the grass will look down at the sky
>   And the pebbles will roll up the stream
> And all men will be good without batting an eye
>   They will make of our earth a dream
> On St. Nevercome's, Nevercome's, Nevercome's Day
>   They will make of our earth a dream

From *The Good Woman of Setzuan,* in *Parables for the Theatre: Two Plays by Bertolt Brecht,* trans. Eric Bentley (New York: Grove Press, 1961), 65.

20. For a splendid presentation of Israel's eschatology, see Donald E. Gowan, *Eschatology in the Old Testament* (Philadelphia: Fortress Press, 1986).

21. Gal. 3:28.

22. I realize that it is almost unseemly for a white homiletician to write on African-American preaching, which is more varied and much more sophisticated than I can possibly know.

23. For an examination of the Black hermenetics, see Warren H. Stewart, Sr., *Interpreting God's Word in Black Preaching* (Valley Forge, PA: Judson Press, 1984).

24. Marc Connelly, *The Green Pastures: A Fable,* in *Representative American Dramas,* ed. M. J. Moses and rev. Joseph Wood Krutch (Boston: Little, Brown and Co., 1941), 823–66.

25. The phrase is from Matthew Lamb, *Solidarity with Victims: Toward a Theology of Social Transformation* (New York: Crossroad, 1982).

26. See the discussion in my *Homiletic* (Philadelphia: Fortress Press, 1987), chapter 16.

27. The so-called "New Hermeneutic," inheriting its models from Heidegger, shunned social meanings as the products of *das Mann* and, instead, preferred to aim texts at an existential self in self-awareness.

28. In sin, obviously, the preservation of an exclusive determinate community can become a "Christian agenda." When such occurs, Christian faith becomes a perversion of its true nature.

29. See Wolfhart Pannenberg, "Hermeneutics and Universal History," in *History and Hermeneutic,* ed. R. W. Funk with G. Ebeling (New York: Harper and Row, 1967), 122–52.

30. See, for example, the argument in Letty M. Russell, *Household of Freedom* (Philadelphia: Westminster Press, 1987).

31. Earlier we distinguished between a vertical eschatology, which may well urge social neglect, and a horizontal eschatology, which may foster social change.

32. See James H. Cone, *The Spirituals and the Blues* (New York: Seabury Press, 1972). Also see Cone's discussion of eschatology in *A Black Theology of Liberation* (New York: J. B. Lippincott, 1970), chapter 7.

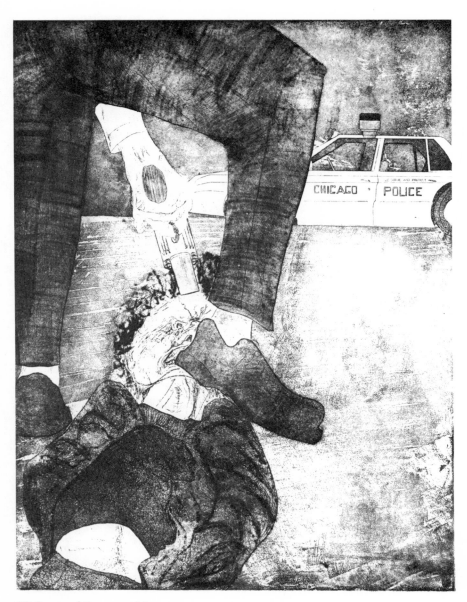

We Serve and Protect, etching

7

Little Man and Big Man

1 KINGS 21

Wallace Charles Smith

In the 1960s there was a poster I loved. It showed a giant with a club over his shoulder walking through an idyllic pasture. The caption said, "Yeah, though I walk through the Valley of Death I will fear no evil because I am the baddest so-and-so in the valley" (expletive deleted).

The great theologian Howard Thurman, in discussing this text, says that ultimately this is the story of a big man and a little man. The big man in the account is Ahab, king of Israel. As the king, Ahab is without question the baddest dude in the valley. Kings in the ancient Near East had the sovereign power of life and death over their subjects. Ahab did not need to bother himself with quorum requirements, machinely precisioned motions, or parliamentary propriety. Like Louis XIV, Ahab could easily say, "L'état c'est moi." I am the state. Ahab is a big man because he is the king.

While in China several years ago, I visited Xian, home of one of the great archaeological finds of the twentieth century, an army of terracotta soldiers and horses. It seems this certain king commissioned the creation of lifelike statues of soldiers and horses to be buried at the entrance to his tomb to protect him in the afterlife. The burial of these thousands of clay soldiers was actually a humanitarian act because before this, the custom was that upon death a king had all his army killed and buried with him. This king saved his soldiers and buried clay images of them instead. One strange footnote, however, is that he did have all the artists who made the soldiers killed.

Kings in the ancient world had absolute power of life and death over their subjects. Ahab, as king of Israel, is a grand monarch. Servants cower when he speaks. Concubines shudder at the sound of his voice. Television crews from "Lifestyles of the Rich and Famous" come for interviews. Because cars have not been invented he does not have a fleet of Rolls Royces, but his chariots all bear designer signatures.

But there is a danger to doing anything unopposed. The danger of living above criticism is that little cracks and flaws in the character may for years go unnoticed. Ahab has a flaw in his personality called covetousness. "Covet" means to wish for enviously or to desire inordinately what belongs to another. Covetousness is not just greed, it is arrogant greed. The Greek word for covetousness is *pleonexia*. *Pleonexia* is an ugly word. Often in classical Greek writings it denoted overreaching ambition with a violent streak. St. John Chrysostom, preaching in the fourth century A.D., said, "There is a great difference between a rich person and covetous person. A person can be rich who has nothing; yet covetous persons can have everything and still be poor. The covetous person is a keeper not a master, a slave not a lord. A covetous person would sooner give away a portion of flesh than . . . give away the slightest measure of that thing coveted."

I have heard of a man who saves his money and once a year rents the biggest Mercedes he can find. He says when he closes the door he hears a terrific bang, not the insignificant bang one hears when closing the door to a small car. When the Mercedes bang is heard, police take roadblocks away, security people salute, servants straighten their attire, and hotel keepers rush to keep.

Ahab may be like one person who said, "I have been poor and rich, and I'll take rich." Ahab is a Mercedes man in Israel, but he is unmindful of the opposition warring in his soul. This big man is out of touch with the termites gnawing at the foundation of his life. Covetous persons never have enough to satisfy themselves, they only have enough to sink themselves.

Standing in the way of the king's desires is a little man with some integrity. Naboth owns the land adjacent to the king's palace. This land is the land Ahab desires. He wants to put a vegetable garden there. Naboth, although a minuscule man, has the bigness and tenacity to stand up for what he believes is right. Ahab approaches Naboth and offers to trade some other land for this land, or to buy it. Naboth refuses because this land is the ancestral home of his family. This land has significance beyond vegetables. This land represents the dreams and hopes of kin.

Even though the world may call us insignificant because we are not rulers and do not have political clout, we must never wear that garment. Naboth knows that even when facing great sovereigns one will only be small if one acts small.

Naboth does what the so-called little and powerless have done since the dawning of civilization. Naboth reminds Ahab that there is power higher than a monarch's authority.

Naboth says to the king, "The Lord forbid that I should sell." This question you are asking me, Naboth says, is not a financial matter, it is a theological matter. Numbers 26:7 says, "So shall not the inheritance of the children of Israel move from tribe to tribe." Ezekiel said, "Moreover, the prince shall not take the people's inheritance." Naboth says to Ahab, "This is not a question of money, this is a question of faith."

If one is a child of God there are certain things that are never for sale. One's integrity is never vendible. One's truthfulness is not saleable. One's devotion to family is not marketable.

A minuscule man named Naboth culls colossal bravery and reminds Ahab that mighty monarchs and powerless sharecroppers all live under the gaze of the everlasting God. Whether affluent or indigent, only those who wait upon the Lord shall renew their strength. Sovereign or servant, "unless the Lord builds the house, those who build it labor in vain." (Ps. 127:1). Big shot of noncaliber. What does the Lord require of thee but to do justice, love mercy, and walk humbly before God? We all live under the gaze of God.

People in twentieth-century America need to hear this word from Naboth. Godless and powerful persons with insatiable appetites for the weak continue to come into the communities of the oppressed. Sometimes they attempt to develop legislation that makes it impossible for historically Black colleges and universities to survive. Other times they sell abandoned houses to rich people for one dollar, and overnight, rat-ridden rowhouses, like Michael Jackson, get face-lifts. Townhouses become priced so high that the poor and elderly can no longer afford to pay taxes in the neighborhoods where they grew up. Godless big shots continue to lurk and stalk the lives of the powerless.

The word needs to go out from our pulpits and places of proclamation: No one can make us small if we have lofty ideals. We may live in poverty, but we can walk with dignity.

Second-class status seeks to entomb dreams. But honesty resuscitates hope. Littleness cannot be our lot if we trust in the One who is our power. A coach told his football team at practice, "We will run a new play today. I want everyone to pull out and go left, and then I want the new man, Jones, who just arrived and is still in the locker room, to run right." The team said, "He'll be killed." But the coach responded, "You haven't seen Jones."

We have on our side the Creator, Redeemer, Sustainer of the whole team. The Unmoved Mover, the Sure Foundation, the Rock in a Weary Hand is on our side. The Sovereign of oceans, earths, and skies is on our side. The One about whom the heavenly chorus sings anthems of praise is on our side. The One for whom four and twenty elders rise from their thrones to say, "Holy, Holy Lord God Almighty"—there is someone on our side!

But then the scene shifts. We now see Ahab's obesity of power has left him with an undernourished soul.

Ahab is on his bed pouting because he cannot have his way. Ahab, the man whose kingship has been painted with dramatic strokes, is now showing insipid colors.

Poor Ahab, a wimp in wolf's clothing. Like the character in *The Wizard of Oz,* a cowardly lion. Ahab is someone who wants to please. He has set up temples in his kingdom to both Yahweh and Baal. He has attempted to create a world where Elijah and Jezebel can at least be civil. Because Ahab tries to please everybody, when things do not go his way he falls apart.

Deep within, for all his bigness, Ahab does not feel that he has much worth. He needs things to make him feel good about himself. It does not matter what we have attained in life, if we do not have God, our lives are but untended vineyards. Climb the highest mountains, cross unnavigable seas, and those ventures leave even the most courageous persons feeling hollow and empty if there is not God in their lives. We spend our days lamenting unattainable vineyards. But with God we have strength to endure storms, power to stand upheavals. We are all forced to face uncertain seas. Oh, my brothers and sisters, one cannot become so large that one can live without God.

Now enters Jezebel. Jezebel is Ahab's alter ego. Unlike Ahab, her covetousness is not for vineyards; her covetousness is for power. And she knows how to use it.

Traditional morality and respect for another's property is immaterial to Jezebel. She is of the opinion that if that is what the king wants, then that is what the king deserves. Those of might deserve what their power will permit.

Brilliant Wall Street financiers are entitled to some insider trading. Monarchs deserve what they are gifted to achieve. Thomas Jefferson had the right to own slaves; it was the universe's payment to him for being born with a philosopher's mind. Plato had already said the whole world would serve philosophers.

The sentimentality of ordinary men and women must never stand in the way of the aspirations of the palace. In his book *The Closing of the American Mind,* Allan Bloom suggests that the fall of the United States began when minority concerns were permitted in the academic curriculum. If one does not stamp out little people, soon little people will have power.

Jezebel says, "Ahab, stop acting like Pee Wee Herman. You are king, all you need to do is take a lesson from the Godfather and make Naboth an offer he can't refuse. Put a severed horse's head in bed with him—he'll get the message." Jezebel gives Ahab a lesson on Machiavelli. Any monarch knows that when there is opposition one must stamp it out quick and fast. If sentimentalities infuse the political structure, little men will get their head and soon we will be humoring natives by awarding them money for the land that we stole. We might even suggest that racism ought to be corrected by affirmative action. We might establish goals and timetables to bring women up to economic parity. Ahab, you must immediately stamp out this little man's insolence. If not, hundreds of thousands of little men and women might be coming to the palace demanding that we give up all the choice land we keep for ourselves.

Jezebel concocts a plot. She says to Ahab, "If the Senate and House of Representatives won't approve, let's call Oliver North, Secord, and Casey and a few other good old boys from the network, and we'll accuse Naboth of blasphemy." Now, considering that Jezebel is already a Baal worshipper, her calling Naboth a blasphemer is like Tammy Faye accusing Bozo the Clown of wearing too much makeup.

Well, Naboth is killed and Ahab prepares to take the vineyard. And just then along comes Elijah. Elijah reminds Ahab that even big shots are under moral authority. Elijah is God's preacher of justice. Elijah is sent by God to tell Ahab that the dogs will lick his blood just as they have Naboth's blood.

One Scripture raised the question, "Is there any word from the Lord?" One word from God that we can always count on is that justice will run down like waters. When we have struggled and worked and our hands are sore and scarred from the work we've begun, there is One who runs quickly to meet us. God understands us and calls us God's own.

The Bible is a handbook of justice. Ahab, the dogs will lick your blood in the same place they licked Naboth's blood. The universe will right itself. Truth pressed to the ground will rise again. This is why people of faith have always sung, "The Lord will make a way somehow." The God who sent an only child to preach life will not give that child to death. The injustice of Good Friday will be followed by the justice of Easter Sunday morning.

And there is one other dimension. Ahab repents. There is still some God in his soul. Ahab is truly sorry for what he has done.

God does not excuse him. Sin is never excused. Our works will follow us. But God shows God's mercy. Because Ahab has humbled himself and repented, the retribution will not fall on him. But what he wants most, he will not have. Ahab wants to please everybody. But for the rest of his time, this man will be hated by his own people. But in spite of his flaws, God will not abandon him.

Naboth may be miniscule by Ahab's standards. He may have no delegates to take with him to the convention. He may have no millionaires to back his campaign for truth, but this politically elfin man demonstrates a resolve that is indomitable.

Like Rosa Parks, he simply says "No." He will not ride in the back seat of the bus. Like the Freedom Fighters, he will not let dogs, guns, or horses keep him from crossing the Edmund Pettus bridge. Naboth may be small, but he has large virtues.

8

A World Transformed
from Greed to Gift

JOEL 2:23–30; LUKE 16:19–31

Gail R. O'Day

No Ball Playing Allowed, etching

The invitation offered by the gospel text is one most of us would probably rather not accept. The parable we have read from Luke is not one that entices us to linger. It has many hard edges: it makes us uncomfortable; it is not readily inspirational. It is perhaps more the stuff that nightmares, not dreams, are made of. Its images are so strong and graphic that we are tempted to avert our eyes. A rich man, clothed in purple and fine linen, eating lavish meals on silver plates. He eats and eats, alone in his own empire. And the other character—a poor man lying at the outside gate of the rich man's house, his body festering with sores, scavenging for whatever scraps the trash collectors drop as they come down the driveway. The neighborhood dogs circle around him, licking his sores. Surplus and lack. Selfishness and need. Comfort and anguish.

The parable does not become any easier when the characters die. The poor man—who has a name (and that is all he has), Lazarus—dies and is carried by the angels to Abraham's bosom. Happily ever after? Perhaps—but he is not the only person Jesus tells us about. The rich man dies, too, and he is buried. He is not welcomed to the bosom of Abraham, however. He is in Hades, in torment. Comfort and anguish again—but inverted. The rich man abused the poor Lazarus in life, and now the rich man suffers. Does this inversion teach him anything? Does he repent of his neglect and abuse?

Sadly and harshly, the answer is "No." The rich man still assumes he has privilege of rank and power, still assumes that Lazarus is at his beck and call: "Father Abraham, have mercy upon me, and send Lazarus to dip the end of his finger in water and cool my tongue; for I am in agony in these flames." He never offered Lazarus a cool drink during life, yet now he expects Lazarus to minister to him, to cool off his tongue.

Abraham's answer is swift and uncompromising—no mercy for you. There is comfort and mercy for Lazarus now, but not for you. The chasm between the rich man and Lazarus in death is just as broad as it was in life—and just as unbridgeable. Only now the two are on opposite sides of the chasm. Comfort and anguish again. In life, the rich man called all the shots while Lazarus suffered. In death, Lazarus is comforted and no one heeds the rich man and his mock show of power.

The rich man makes one more appeal to Abraham, however: Send Lazarus to tell my brothers. The rich man still does not get it. He still thinks Lazarus should be his servant: If Lazarus cannot come to me, at least let him go to my brothers. I am a rich man; my brothers are rich men; listen to me, Abraham. Make the poor man serve us.

You can almost hear Abraham laugh when he answers this time—or perhaps you can almost hear him cry. Once again, Abraham's answer is no mercy: "They have Moses and the prophets; they should listen to them." They have all they need. Let them hear and understand. But Moses and the prophets seem inadequate to the rich man. He wants something more stupendous, something so out of the ordinary that it will break through his brothers' self-interest. Abraham will not be moved, however. Moses and the prophets are enough. Because if the rich man's brothers do not recognize Moses and the prophets, "neither will they be convinced even if someone rises from the dead."

End of the story. But how can it be? Are there not a few more verses somewhere, is there not something to soften Abraham's relentlessness? Is there not an offer of mercy somewhere? No. The story ends as harshly as it began, perhaps more so. The only mercy offered is that which has been offered all along—that found in Moses and the prophets. And if we cannot find God's mercy and word there, do not expect to find it in someone who rises from the dead. Even Jesus, the crucified and risen One, offers no escape from the harshness of this parable.

The world this text invites us into is a world of pain, greed, brokenness, human failure, sin. The rich man is in torment because he could hear neither the prophets nor Moses nor Abraham. He did not know, he could not hear, that his power and wealth and oppression of other people were against the will of God. He did not know that God longs for God's creation to be whole, and that his selfish actions stood in the way of that wholeness.

The world of this parable, then, is a broken world, a wounded world, in which relationships and creation are out of sync. But the Bible readings also invite us into another world—the world invoked by Joel. The world of the Joel text is as joyous as that of the parable is bleak. The world of Joel is a healed world, a redeemed world, a world of God's peace and comfort. Luke invites us to the brokenness of creation; Joel invites us to the abundant health of creation. Luke invites us to anguish; Joel invites us to comfort. Could we use Joel's invitation, then, to cancel out Luke's and thereby avoid all the hard places in the parable? Are the two invitations—and the two worlds they evoke—mutually exclusive?

The answer is "No," because the two texts, Joel and Luke, are really the flip side of the same world. Both invite us into the world of God's love for the poor, of God's compassion for creation, but they invite us from different sides. One, the Luke text, invites us into God's world of compassion from the side of human pain and human resistance. The other, the Joel text, invites us into God's world of care for the needy from the side of God's graciousness.

Think about the Joel text. What God supplies to Israel is an indication of what Israel was lacking. God offers rain, grain, oil, wine, relief from the plague of locusts, abundant food, the end of shame, and the gift of God's spirit. God is generous beyond anything Israel could imagine. What has been missing for Israel—food, shelter, livelihood, human dignity—is what is missing for Lazarus. Think of the land without rain, with dry and parched fields, with vineyards that yield no fruit. Think of the land overrun by locusts. Think of the people without God's Spirit. The picture is as painful as that of Lazarus, lying at the gate, his open sores licked by dogs.

There is something wrong in a world where people like Lazarus lie hungry in the streets. There is something wrong in a world where people and livestock die of thirst, where fields yield no grain. There is something wrong in a world where the wealthiest 3 percent of the population has more money than the bottom 25 percent. There is something wrong in a world where the rallying cry of "no taxes" is really a cover for the abdication of even the most basic social services and responsibilities. When we, like the rich man in the parable, isolate ourselves from the needs of others, there is something wrong.

God knows about that wrong, and so in the Joel text, we are offered a vision of a restored world. Israel has been like the rich man of the Lucan parable—oblivious to Moses and the prophets, forgetful that God's promises are for all of God's creation. But in Joel, we see that God's graciousness, God's compassion and generosity outrun our own selfishness, our own interests that pervert God's creation. In Joel, the chasm that separates Lazarus from the rich man is bridged. God's gift makes creation whole.

Where does that leave us? As we think about the parched places of the world, the destitute places of our cities, how can we move away from the brokenness of creation, embodied in parable of the rich man and Lazarus, to the signs of plenty and wholeness in Joel? How can we

move from drought to abundance, from starvation to food, from anguish to comfort, from greed to gift?

There is only one way, and it lies in the last gift promised by God
in Joel:

*Then afterward I will pour out my spirit on all flesh; your sons
and your daughters shall prophesy, your old men shall dream
dreams, and your young men shall see visions. Even on the male
and female slaves, in those days, I will pour out my spirit.*

The gift of God's Spirit. With God's Spirit, we are empowered to
believe in God's restoration of creation. We are empowered to imagine
moving beyond the world of Lazarus and the rich man. We are empowered to imagine a world in which the abundance of the Joel text becomes a reality for all. The gift of God's Spirit empowers us to follow
our visions, to work for our dreams. And so, workers for Habitat for
Humanity gather to build homes for strangers. And churches provide
job-training and rehabilitation programs for the homeless and unemployed, so that lives of scarcity can be transformed to lives of abundance. And people raise their voices in unceasing calls for economic justice. Such actions are signs, small ones perhaps, when we think of the
task before us, but signs nonetheless that God's Spirit is at work in us to
bring about a new social order.

With the love of God's Spirit, we are empowered to affirm God's
love for the poor and God's hopes for the poor. And we are empowered
to act, despite the odds and the cost, out of that love and those hopes.
The gift of God's Spirit empowers us to affirm God's desires that the
poor and the needy—and all of us—live in a restored creation. The visions and dreams of which the Joel text sings are of a time when sharing
by all will mean scarcity for none.

Without God, such a restored world will not be possible. We need
only remember the rich man in the parable who could not or would not
hear the word of God. But with God, with the words of Moses and the
prophets, with God's outpoured Spirit, in the presence of the One who
was raised from the dead, the vats shall overflow with wine and oil.
With God's Spirit, we shall all—Lazarus included—eat in plenty and be
satisfied, and the time of rejoicing will never end.

9

Gospel Lite

June Alliman Yoder

Polish Woman on El, lithograph

One of my seminary students recently preached a sermon entitled "Gospel Lite." The point of the sermon was that we actually want to hear sermons that are one-third less challenging than the regular gospel. He suggested that serious Bible study has gotten us down. We spend our hours researching a text only to produce a sermon that no one wants to hear. The message of the Scripture seems at odds with our own lifestyles. And so he offered Gospel Lite—one-third less challenging.

He included such excerpts as "Jesus died for our errors in judgment," and "She who would be my disciple must hop in her Honda and follow me," and "Blessed are the rich for they must be doing something right," and "Love your enemies while killing them," and "He who hates his life should see a good psychiatrist."

So get your congregation off your back; tell them what they want to hear with Gospel Lite. You'll sleep better at night, too. Order now. Dial 1-800-THE-WORD and you can get Gospel Lite for just $9.95.

Thank goodness Gospel Lite is not available in stores and, we hope, not in many seminaries. But in a certain sense Gospel Lite is preferred by us all. In the New Testament Jesus spends most of his earthly ministry trying to beat Gospel Lite out of the disciples. The Messiah wasn't going to suffer; he would rule and they would rule with him. The Epistles too are full of warnings regarding deceivers and anti-Christs. The temptation is to water down and pervert the gospel. And there is nothing new about it.

Once upon a time, not so long ago and not far away at all, a woman came to Jesus and asked, "Professor, what good things must I do if I want to get eternal life?" Jesus replied to her, "Why do you ask me about what is good? There is only One who is good. If you want to enter life, obey the commandments."

"Well, professor, which ones?" the woman asked. She was eager to know and bright-eyed about it all. Jesus replied, "Do not murder. Do not commit adultery. Do not steal. Do not give false witness. Honor your father and mother. And love your neighbor as yourself." "That is just wonderful," the woman replied, "for all of these I have kept. No problem."

And she began to enumerate in her mind how successfully she had kept all of these commandments. "Do not murder." Indeed, she had never killed anybody. She was one of those people who would escort a spider from the house to freedom in the grass. She was one who would rescue a chipmunk from the mouth of a cat who had so playfully and triumphantly presented it to her. She was one who had done several days' duty for women's peace movements. She was one who was always encouraging children not to play with guns. Indeed, she not only had never committed murder, she was pro-peace in the best sense of the word. No wonder she was pleased when Jesus replied, "Do not murder."

"Do not commit adultery." She had been fairly successful here, too. One wonderful husband in her life. The only man in her life. And though there had been struggles in their marriage, it was a good marriage and she was happy to be married to her husband. She was not like the woman at the well who was on husband number whatever, she was not the Zsa Zsa Gabor of her neighborhood. Indeed, she was a faithful wife. And she smiled when she heard Jesus say, "You shall not commit adultery."

"Do not steal." Of course not. Why would you steal? She had adequate funds to pay for everything she needed. There was no reason to steal. Though she had been tempted when she was four or five years old to take some licorice from the supermarket, she had eventually paid for it. Her good conscience had kept her on the straight and narrow. Still today, in fact, when the clerk recently gave her too much change at the supermarket, she offered it back. She didn't steal when it was given to her. And so no wonder she smiled when Jesus said, "You shall not steal."

"Do not give false testimony." Ah yes, false testimony. She sometimes had trouble understanding the difference between truth and honesty. She sometimes bent honesty, but truth remained firm. Truth was a big deal with her. She was committed to bottom-line truth. And if in a difficult situation you had to tell a half-truth in order to make someone comfortable, she could certainly understand that. But she was not one who was given to anything but truth. Truth was part of life that she carried deep inside her. And so it was no wonder that she was pleased when Jesus said, "Do not give false testimony or bear false witness."

"Honor your father and mother." Again she smiled, for she had been a parent pleaser since she was a little girl. She had always done everything she could to please Mom and Dad. And now, as a middle-aged woman, she was still doing all that she could to please them. She was anticipating caring for them in their aging years. She invited her husband's widowed mother for dinner every week. She was doing a good job, she thought, in honoring her parents, in doing that which made them proud and grateful for having had such children as she.

"Love your neighbor as yourself." She was good at this one, too. Just this week she had taken food into the garden-sharing program at the church. She had preached at the jail. And a few weeks ago, as she was checking out at the grocery counter, the lady in front of her had discovered that she had too little money and was having to choose which of her items to put back. She had graciously paid the rest of that lady's grocery bill so that she could take all of her food home. Yes, she loved her neighbors. She loved her neighbors as herself.

And so it was no wonder that she smiled when Jesus rattled off this list of things she must do if she was to get eternal life. She answered him, "All these I have kept. What do I still lack?"

Jesus responded, "If you want to be perfect, if you want eternal life, go sell your possessions and give to the poor—and you will have treasure in heaven. Then come and follow me."

When the woman heard this, when *I* heard this, I went away sad because I had great wealth. Amen.

10

Cry for Justice, Reap the Spirit

Acts 6:1–6

Jorge L. Morales

Bull Session, etching

Since the beginning of time, we humans have had to create institutions and structured society. We have organized ourselves and created vehicles to meet particular needs, and as we build these institutions we also develop the criteria by which one becomes a member of a particular body.

This is the case also with the church. Though the church has an organizational structure and functions as an institution, it is also to be free to be empowered by the Holy Spirit. It is to allow the incorporation of others, to be open to the new, and to welcome all to share the benefits and responsibilities, assuring the Reign of God.

There was an incident in the primitive church that points first to the church's temptation to marginalize some of its members and then to its openness to all by the power and grace of God. The first Christians

124

were Palestinian Jews who had converted to Christianity. The language, culture, politics, economy, and the whole Judaic self-concept as "God's people" or the "chosen" played important roles in identifying who could be a Christian and benefit from the privilege of being part of the church.

The first six verses of the sixth chapter of Acts refer to an incident in which a group of persons charge that they are not receiving just treatment. The text reveals the discrimination that was present in the church and the action taken to resolve the issue:

About this time, when the number of disciples was increasing, the Hellenists made a complaint against the Hebrews: in the daily distribution their own widows were overlooked. So the twelve called a full meeting of the disciples and addressed them, "It would not be right for us to neglect the word of God so as to give out food; you brothers must select from among yourselves seven men of good reputation, filled with the spirit, and with wisdom; we will hand over this duty to them and continue to devote ourselves to prayer and to service of the word." The whole assembly approved of this proposal and elected Stephen, a man full of faith and of the Holy Spirit, together with Philip, Prochorus, Nicanor, Timon, Parmenas, and Nicalaus of Antioch, a convert to Judaism. They presented these to the Apostles, who prayed and laid their hands on them. (Jerusalem Bible)

The Hebrews mentioned are the Palestinian Jews who spoke Aramaic. They held most of the decision-making power in the church, and therefore the problem or complaint of the Hellenists was directed at them. The congregation was made up of both Palestinian Jews and Hellenists. It is important to note that the Hellenists were also Jews, but they lived outside of Palestine, had been influenced by the Greek culture, spoke the Greek language, and had adapted to Greek customs. Aid to the widows was the issue that was brought forth, but no doubt there were other serious differences because of the distinction between the two groups. Language could have been a major issue.

The distribution of food was a Jewish tradition that had been carried over into Christianity. The poor were taken care of by a daily dole from the funds made available by the consecrated Christians (cf. 2:44–45, 4:32–37). The number of disciples had increased. The apostles were apparently too busy with their appointed role of preaching the Word to attend sufficiently to giving out food. The task of the distribution had been given to some disciples who were seeing only to the needs of the Palestinian widows and ignoring the Hellenists.

The matter was of major importance to the apostles. It was important that the church defend the values of the Reign that Jesus had proclaimed and stated was in their midst. The early Christian community had to reflect these values. In Acts 4:32–34 the community reflects the success of the ethic of the Reign of God:

The whole group of believers was united, heart and soul; no one claimed for his own use anything that he had, as everything they owned was held in common. The Apostles continued to testify to the resurrection of the Lord Jesus with great power and they were all given great respect. None of their members was ever in want, as all those who owned land or houses would sell them, and bring the money from them to present it to the Apostles; it was then distributed to any member who might be in need. (Jerusalem Bible)

The neglect of the Hellenist widows was a serious violation of these values. It would put at risk the purpose of the church as the true community that is to reflect the biblical concept of the people of God— the Kingdom of God on earth.

The Hellenists were part of the Christian community, yet they were objects of discrimination and were treated as outsiders. So they were moved to action; they challenged the apostles to see that justice was done. The plight of the widows, who were already destitute, was made worse by discrimination. The Hellenists knew well the tradition of distribution, even if they were not observing all the customs the Hebrews deemed necessary. They wanted respect and equal treatment. Religious prejudice and discrimination should have no place in the church, and the Hellenists were the first in the primitive church to stand and defend themselves against it.

The apostles were men of great wisdom and wanted to correct this injustice. Their method of resolving the matter points to their desire for the church to be an institution of all the people. They gathered the whole congregation and made a proposal.

The Twelve asked the group to select seven among them to whom the duty of administering the relief to the widows would be given. The conditions set by the Twelve (v. 3) were that those chosen be of "good reputation, filled with the Spirit and with wisdom." The selection of the seven may have been made to satisfy the Hellenists and to avoid further difficulties. The whole congregation seemed to have been in agreement with the proposition, and the seven were selected. This points to the fact that the Hellenists had good cause to complain and to get what they had a right to receive as part of the church.

Though these seven have been referred to as deacons, elders, presbyters, etc., it appears that they, especially Stephen and Philip, held a unique office somewhat parallel to the Apostolate. After their election they are portrayed not as table servers but as much more—as great evangelists. The Twelve who insisted that they must devote all their time to "prayer and the ministry of the word" were slow to see that with God there is no discrimination between persons. Stephen, Philip, and five others were mundane enough to be assigned table-serving jobs, but somehow they developed keen insight into the gospel and provided the leadership for a Christianity that is truly spiritual rather than legal, that embraces humanity rather than just a nation.

The apostles initiated a process by which the Hellenists came to have leaders sensitive to their particular language and cultural needs. Persons who could understand their view of the gospel. Apostles of their own. The Twelve not only recommended a process of election but also, as responsible, Spirit-filled leaders, proposed a solution that carried with it the power for the Hellenists to resolve their own particular needs. It was an appointment with power. The seven became for the Hellenists what the Twelve had been to the Palestinians. What qualified the seven was their faithfulness and commitment to the church. When the apostles "prayed and laid hands on them," no charisma was transmitted. The seven already possessed the Holy Spirit. The act was a formal symbol of appointment to the task to which they were already elected by God.

While the Palestinian Jews had the power to make major decisions in the primitive church, the Hellenist Jews were not completely powerless. Like many discriminated-against minorities in our time, they had

God, who is on the side of the poor. They had their voices and their right to complain and to protest and denounce injustice. This cry of injustice can be heard in our time—within the church but most often outside it. The cry comes from those who are victims of both the church and unjust social structures. From inside and outside the church we hear those who cry out and we see those who respond with liberating actions, and in both we witness the presence of the Spirit.

The acts of the Hellenists, of the Twelve, and of the whole congregation were empowering and beneficial to all who partook of the Reign of God. The complaints of the Palestinian Jews, the response of the Hellenist Jews, were acts of faith that led to gain for the whole church.

Stephen and Philip were two of the greatest evangelists of the early church. Stephen devoted himself totally to the work of the church and became the first Christian martyr, defending his belief to the very end. He proclaimed "the way" to his last breath. Although he did not set forth as Paul did, to convert Gentiles, he declared that Christianity could not be limited to the Jews. He opened the gates and marked the transition of the church from Jewish to Gentile Christianity. The persecution that followed his death led to the dispersion of the disciples and thus the promulgation of the gospel to the Samaritans and the Gentile world. His followers also scattered to Phoenicia, Cyprus, and Antioch (11:19–21).

It was in Antioch that foreign missions began and where the disciples were first called Christians. The Antioch church, founded by persecuted Jews after the death of Stephen, a man chosen to administer relief, later sent relief to Jerusalem at a time of famine and promoted the gospel throughout the world.

Philip preached and healed at Samaria (8:4–6), led Simon the Sorcerer to become an active believer in Christ (8:9–13), and was instrumental in bringing about the conversion of an Ethiopian and a eunuch on the staff of Queen Candace to Judaism (8:26–29). His deeds continued and included proclaiming Christ's message to northeastern Africa and raising four daughters who had the gift of prophecy (21:91).

The poor, people of color, women, and other minorities today challenge the church to live up to the values of God's Reign. Some in our churches believe that because they have been members for a long time, the church belongs to them. The presence of the poor, of Asians, of Blacks, or of Hispanics is seen as an intrusion that threatens what they perceive as privileges that come with seniority. In God's Reign, in the church, there is no system of seniority. On the contrary, "the last shall be first." Those who have been Christians longest must be open to learning from latecomers. The history of the latecomers is also a part of the history and tradition of God's people. Their stories, sense of community, values, etc., are not liabilities but gifts from God. The gifts of those whose culture, language, and racial background are different from those of the dominant group can contribute to a more just and humane society, furthering the establishment of the Reign Jesus proclaimed and was crucified to initiate. As an institution the church must be open to the challenges of our time. How it responds to these challenges determines the degree to which it is truly an instrument of God's saving and liberating grace.

The election of the seven would have not taken place had it not been for the fact that a group of Hellenists would not allow an act of discrimination to continue but challenged an institution to change its unjust practices against the poor and oppressed widows. Their election was a response to a protest that led to the empowerment of great pillars in the history and development of the primitive church. Given the opportunity, representatives of discriminated minorities today can also become great evangelists, heroes of the Christian faith, and builders of God's Reign.

Notes on Contributors

Brian Bakke is the resident artist at the Lighthouse Art Center, a subsidiary of Uptown Urban Impact, Inc., in Chicago. He is also the director of community relations and advocate in community affairs at Uptown Baptist Church, Chicago. Mr. Bakke lives in the part of Chicago known as "the Corridor," a two-block-wide, two-mile-long strip of densely populated depressed housing and commerce. The scenes of his art come from his home and church neighborhoods. Mr. Bakke exhibited many of his works during the 1990 Niebuhr Conference on the Church and Society.

David G. Buttrick is an ordained minister of the Presbyterian church. He has spoken at ministers' conferences and church assemblies in more than thirty states and has written or edited nine books, including his award-winning *Homiletic*, and more than one hundred articles. Since 1982 he has been a professor of homiletics and liturgics at the Divinity School of Vanderbilt University.

James H. Cone has written more than one hundred articles and nine books, the most recent of which is *Martin & Malcom & America*. He has lectured in dozens of countries and at some three hundred colleges across America. He is the Briggs Distinguished Professor of Theology at Union Theological Seminary in New York, where he has taught since 1969.

Greg J. Duncan has written more than one hundred articles and five books. At the University of Michigan, with which he has been associated since 1972, he is the program director and research scientist at the Survey Research Center, a co-director of the Panel Study of Income Dynamics project, and a professor of economics.

Ronald Goetz has written more than 150 articles, lectures widely to Chicago-area groups, and preaches on alternating weekends to his local United Church of Christ congregation. Since 1986 he has held the Niebuhr Distinguished Chair of Theology and Ethics at Elmhurst College, where he has taught since 1963.

Jacquelyn Grant has published numerous articles and a recent book, *White Women's Christ and Black Women's Jesus: Feminist Christologies and Womanist Response.* Since 1980 she has been at the Interdenominational Theological Center in Atlanta, where she is an associate professor of systematic theology.

Martha S. Hill is a co-director of the Panel Study of Income Dynamics project and senior study director of the Survey Research Center of the University of Michigan.

Saul D. Hoffman is a professor of economics at the University of Delaware.

Jorge L. Morales is the immediate past president of Centro Para Desarrollo Comunitario Y Liberato (Center for Community and Leadership Development). He is a published author, an adjunct professor of theology at Elmhurst College, and the pastor of the First Congregational Church of Chicago. He is a respected and effective activist in that city's Hispanic community.

Gail R. O'Day, an ordained minister of the United Church of Christ, has published three books and numerous articles. She is an associate professor of biblical preaching at Candler School of Theology, Emory University, where she has served since 1987.

Paul Plenge Parker, an active member of The Mennonite Church, is an assistant professor at Elmhurst College, where he has taught ethics since 1987. He is the program director for Elmhurst College's Niebuhr Conference on the Church and Society and works closely with the Lombard Mennonite Peace Center. His areas of specialization are racism, poverty, and violence.

Wallace Charles Smith is a published author, an adjunct professor of preaching at the Divinity School of Vanderbilt University, and the pastor of the First Baptist Church, Capitol Hill, Nashville.

June Alliman Yoder, an ordained minister in The Mennonite Church, is a writer, public speaker (often called the Erma Bombeck of The Mennonite Church), and professor of communication and preaching at the Associated Mennonite Biblical Seminaries in Goshen, Indiana.